DEALING WITH GRIEF, THEIRS AND OURS

Dealing with Grief, Theirs and Ours

Jeroid O'Neil Roussell, Jr., D.Min.

ALBA·HOUSE NEW·YORK

SOCIETY OF ST. PAUL, 2187 VICTORY BLVD., STATEN ISLAND, NEW YORK 10314

Library of Congress Cataloging-in-Publication Data

Roussell, Jeroid O'Neil.
Dealing with grief, theirs and ours / Jeroid O'Neil Roussell, Jr.
p. cm.
Includes bibliographical references.
ISBN 0-8189-0823-8
1. Church work with the bereaved. I. Title
BV4330.R68 1999
259'.6 — dc21 99-17443
CIP

Produced and designed in the United States of America by the Fathers and Brothers of the Society of St. Paul, 2187 Victory Boulevard, Staten Island, New York 10314, as part of their communications apostolate.

Printing Information:

Current Printing - first digit 1 2 3 4 5 6 7 8 9 10

Year of Current Printing - first year shown

1999 2000 2001 2002 2003 2004 2005 2006 2007

ACKNOWLEDGMENTS

Grateful acknowledgment to my wife,
Sheila O'Connell-Roussell,
for her editing of the final manuscript and
encouragement during its writing.

PREFACE

How This Book Came About

After years of encountering grief in my work at the hospital, in a prison, as a teacher, at the parish level and in my private practice as a pastoral counselor and spiritual director, I still felt the need for a better grasp and understanding of the mysterious stages of grief. I naively thought that through increased knowledge I could "conquer grief." In the ensuing process of study and research, I became captivated in a very personal way by the topic and began to focus on my own issues of grief and mortality. Coming face to face with my own mortality, I came to realize that there was Someone greater who was involved in my life and in the lives of those whom I encountered.

What started out for me as an academic study in which I had an emotional interest opened the door to new personal discoveries and relationships. Entering into the joys and sorrows of others, I experienced in a profound way the richness of people's lives as they shared with me their experiences, feelings, thoughts and insights. Together we were able to analyze our common encounters with grief to discover a compassionate God mysteriously loving us through them all.

I have been privileged to journey with many, many people over the years. In the situations discussed in this book, I have changed important facts and combined experiences in order to honor confidentiality. My ministerial approach involves a vision of spiritual and emotional care that connects various pastoral resources with the goal of integrating these into the lives of caring persons.

In Chapter One, I map out my assumptions for this grief and bereavement ministry. Standing behind our ministry, giving meaning to our queries about life and death, is God (present within), the source of strength and inspiration for all caregivers. The spiritual and pastoral dimensions of care are not secondary, but central, to the medical, psychological, and social aspects of care.

In Chapter Two we see grief from a (w)holistic perspective including normal and abnormal aspects with a movement toward recovery and transformation. Both loss and grief are integral to human experience. We are challenged to find ways to journey through the process of grief to attain completion.

Chapter Three develops a biblical/theological perspective which informs our understanding of human experience. As a Christian, I have chosen to develop a theology of incarnation, cross/suffering, and hope/resurrection as the underlying basis for caring in times of loss.

Chapter Four will lead caregivers to grow in spiritual transformation through centering on the interior dimension which focuses on the image of God in self and others. Caregivers are called to be conveyers of an ever deepening and expanding spiritual transformation process of personal and client growth.

In Chapter Five, I draw together my reflections for ministry, connecting some of the emphases developed in earlier chapters, and invite the reader to join me in the challenge — and to be energized — in caring for the caregiver.

The appendices follow the five chapters. Appendix A lays out pastoral resources for grief ministers. Caregivers are led to evaluate the quality of their empathy, respect and genuineness toward others through reflection questions and/or discussion with others. Through spiritual and pastoral assessment, through reflection on personal issues surrounding death, caregivers embrace a greater sense of self and enhance their ability to assist people in the throes of death and dying.

This section includes role playing and a guided imagery

exercise as valuable resources. Appendix B shares reflections about perspectives on death. Appendix C describes how pastoral care volunteers are caregiver resources. I detail a guided meditation exercise combined with suggestions for the use of melodic and healing music. Appendix D is a descriptive annotated bibliography on pastoral literature. Appendix E is an annotated bibliography of books and articles which are useful resources. Next, the notes follow for Chapters One, Two, Three, Four and Five. After these references, the notes follow for Appendices A and C.

I hope these materials will empower individuals to develop healthy ways of dealing with their mortality, coping with both the losses and gains of their life. Through this pastoral process people will appropriate a greater awareness of their unique spirituality through the recognition of the need to care for oneself and others in a (w)holistic manner. This pastoral material seeks to stimulate people to live their personal vision in their lives and caregiving.

TABLE OF CONTENTS

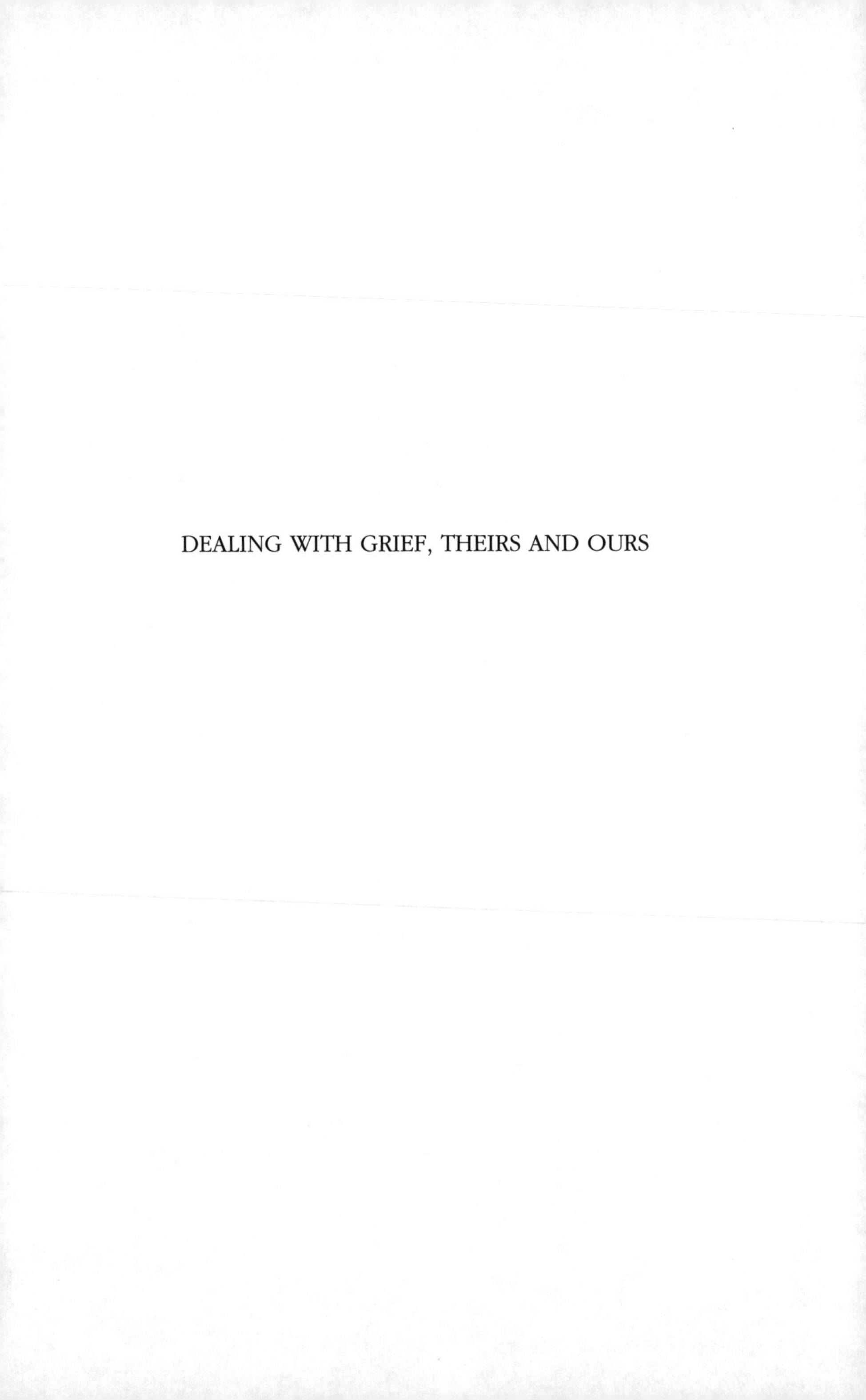

DEALING WITH GRIEF, THEIRS AND OURS

Chapter One

GRIEF AND BEREAVEMENT MINISTRY

Purpose

Recently I was talking to a friend who was aware that I worked as a chaplain. He was trying to catch up on what I had been doing for the last year. I began to tell him about this book I was writing at this time. When I mentioned the topic, *Dealing With Grief, Theirs and Ours*, he looked at me with a stare of puzzlement and dismay. He said, "Why would you want to do that?" As I began to explain my desire to look at loss and grief within my experience, he stiffened his shoulders and body while changing the subject. Grief is not the preferred topic for dinner party conversation. But whatever one may feel about loss and grief, they are a fact of human life.

As a hospital chaplain, I observe many situations and varieties of loss and grief. Sometimes people experience loss just by being in the hospital — and they would rather be anywhere else. As people come face to face with their physical vulnerabilities they decide whether they will acknowledge or ignore them. When people experience the death of a friend, they are suddenly thrust into the fear, the confusion, the pain and the suffering of this loss. One may cope with the loss or deny it using a variety of styles and possibilities, or one may choose to connect and discover its meaning.

Loss and grief do not stop at the hospital door; it is part of the human condition. Developmental transitions, a job change or a move to another locale, the devastation or relief that comes from divorce or separation from one's spouse, dysfunctional family issues, drugs or alcohol abuse can enflame any situation. Arguments, yelling, screaming and/or violence can bring on crises affecting the loss of self-esteem and a sense of worth. Today the caregiver encounters a broad spectrum of situations that produce grief. One may offer care to those processing the loss of a job, a home, a spouse, a title, or the ravages of sexual and mental abuse. Loss and grief are present in all human institutions and aspects of life.

People respond to loss in different ways. Some respond in a stoic and somewhat distant fashion while others do so in a warm and more sympathetic manner to another's grief. Some choose to sit quietly with their loved ones, while others yell or express their feelings in very demonstrative ways. Some join support groups to talk and share with others who validate their experience. Some look for help in religious reading materials and spend extra time in prayer. Others work harder, jog and exercise on a regular basis. Some kick back and let life coast by, not getting uptight about their losses or simply denying them.

Working in critical or trauma situations, the first priority of healthcare workers is to take care of any medical or psychological problems they themselves may have, e.g., denying or repressing their own grief in order to function in a professional manner. To be of help to others, they must be able at times to set aside personal feelings while developing appropriate means to express their emotions in a healthy way. This book will offer skills for dealing in healthful ways with one's emotions so that caregivers can become more comfortable with their own and others' experiences of loss and grief.

Basic Assumptions

Grief and bereavement ministry challenge us to view life and its limitations realistically. In the context of a personal, dynamic and (w)holistic approach, care providers are asked to reflect on their own personal and professional ways of coping with loss and grief. To view all aspects of one's life — with its shadows, vulnerabilities, weaknesses, possibilities, skills and strengths — opens one to a high degree of empathy for the suffering of others and facilitates quality personal and professional caregiving.

As a lay Catholic hospital chaplain working in a collaborative team approach with nurses, physicians, ancillary staff, lay pastors, chaplains, volunteers, community ministers and other clergy, I have learned that spiritual care can no longer be, if it ever was, the sole domain of the chaplain, clergy, ordained minister or priest. Teachers, campus ministers, pastoral administrators, parish ministers, youth workers, aunts, uncles, moms and dads, brothers and sisters and even classmates are all caregivers who can function as channels of healing. All are called to offer compassion and to help those who are bearing the Cross of suffering to discover beyond it the Resurrection and the hope it offers.

Theological, Pastoral, and Personal Reflections

We must not be afraid to listen to what our own emotional agony and pain are telling us. Only then can we hope to be able to hear what another is suffering and help them through it. Those who reflect and evaluate their own feelings generated by comparable situations in their own life prepare themselves to empathize with others.[1]

If we want to help persons in their grief, the caregiver needs a "capacity for reflective review" of their own personal loss and grief.[2]

When people have difficulty reflecting on their own life

experiences, they put up walls and barriers between themselves and others. An example of this is seen in the movie *Beaches*. C.C. Bloom (Bette Midler) does not really hear her best friend, Hilary Whitney (Barbara Hershey), who is dying of heart disease and tries to share her feelings about her not being able to raise her young daughter:[3]

Hilary Whitney: I'm the one who won't live to see my daughter grow into a woman, who won't be able to protect her from the world; and I hate it, I hate it, that she would rather be with you. Who has energy, who's fun!...
I don't want it to be over with, yet. You don't understand what it feels like, all right. You're still in the land of the living.

C.C. Bloom: Well so are you. You are not dead yet. So, stop living as if you are![4]

C.C. walks away in a defensive huff not hearing her friend's fear and pain. She is caught in a self-centered world, void of any real connection with her friend's suffering, and a profound opportunity for caring and hope is missed.

The effective caregiver needs to be aware of who they are as persons. Our values, attitudes, and beliefs about life define us. All too often biases are transmitted through nonverbal behavior. This may hinder our ability to understand what another person is trying to communicate. Our biases deafen us, permitting us to hear only those things which lie within our own frame of reference.[5] If we continue to grow we become reflective persons aware of our own inner experience even while we are being attentive to others. Developing a keen intuitive and theological sense of people's inner world, we accept the challenge to continual personal reflection and the acquisition of the latest skills in clinical practice.

There is a rich relationship between the practice of pastoral care and counseling, and our biblical heritage. Insights from this heritage enlighten, inform and guide the practice of these pastoral arts, allowing them to become incarnate in our human relationships — illuminated and tested in the arena of human struggle and growth! It is in this sense that pastoral care and counseling are ways of doing theology.[6]

We skew the relationship between our biblical tradition and pastoral counseling when we have not integrated the two. By using each in a literal or myopic fashion, by offering platitudes, pat answers or techniques, we do harm. In a true counseling relationship, we struggle with people about certain basic theological issues on a deeply personal level. Whether the issues are identified by theological labels or not — and in our secularized culture they often are not — the "God" questions and concerns are at the heart of all effective caring and counseling.[7]

Our challenge as pastoral care providers is to integrate theological and psychological realities, bringing together the insights of both in our diagnostic assessments and pastoral action.[8]

The heart of our uniqueness as caregivers lies in our theological and pastoral heritage, orientation, resources and awareness — our spirituality is our frame of reference and the arena of our expertise in action. The awareness that the transpersonal Spirit of God is the core of all reality profoundly influences everything we do.[9] In the words of Dietrich Bonhoeffer, "God is the 'beyond' in the midst of our life."[10]

Denial and Death

In the film *Dying Young*, Miss O'Neill (Julia Roberts) interviews for a position to care for a 28-year-young man, Victor (Campbell Scott) — a leukemia patient. In the explanation of his disease, he paints a picture of the chemotherapy treatment which gives the impression that having cancer is no big deal.[11]

A few scenes later, Victor comes back from the hospital and is extremely sick. The physical horror of the treatment takes him to the point of throwing up, being nauseated and having chills and pains throughout his body. As Miss O'Neill cares for him she experiences something totally different from the sanitized, mild explanation given at the job interview. Victor's narrative description failed to do justice to the ugliness and suffering of what really takes place during his cancer treatments.[12] The same is true of those suffering from grief.

People deal with grief in various ways. One way to come to terms with loss is to deny its existence. It is easier to say, "everything is all right," than to admit what is really happening. We learn to dismiss the telltale signs of grief and we plead ignorance. We turn the other way rather than enter the loss.

Our culture is largely death-denying and death-defying. We tend to isolate and leave the grief-stricken emotionally unsupported. The natural and usual feelings that come with grief seem to be rejected as inappropriate,[13] as we hide from the fear.

In a culture of denial a person's altered affective state is not accepted as part of normal human experience. Our culture does not encourage us to share our uncomfortable feelings. To recognize the general nature and impact of acute grief and to articulate our concern is an attempt at significant and compassionate communication.

A woman whose husband has just died sobs and says, "I'll miss him so very much." The parish minister standing with her responds, "Yes, this is a great loss for you." She places her hand on the wife's shoulder in comfort. The feelings are expressed in this safe place. The parish minister gives this woman permission to acknowledge and express her emotions.[14]

Our culture discourages us to connect with our inner selves. We think it easier to let what is hidden and unknown remain unnoticed. But actually this culture of denial locks the pain deep within us. We are then at the mercy of the pain which may flare up uncontrollably at the most inopportune time. Grief and bereavement ministry helps us to face these denials and to accept our little daily dyings and ultimate death. In acceptance, we find that we can be truly free and move beyond the pain.[15]

In the beginning, denial seems easier than confronting our fears and anxieties. People are uncomfortable facing the unknown. Separation from familiar persons and places causes a special anxiety,[16] but health demands truth.

We've all seen how the pattern works. One spouse denies that he/she is tired and does not want to go out dancing. But she/he goes out to please the other partner and does not have a good time. A middle-aged man picks up a heavy box because he does not want to be shown up by a younger man. He knows he should not because his back is already in pain. Still he does it and pulls a muscle. When we are true to our feelings we'll be better able to love life and enjoy our relationships more fully.

Death anxiety produces another form of denial. Here a person repudiates the prevalent sense of fear, yet one's fantasy abounds with mixed ambivalent images. The images and fears of death are there. They are part of the person and yet foreign too. On an unconscious level, the individual tends to respond with outright negativity[17] and rejects the possibility that fearing death could be a part of his/her existence. It's just not possible in any fashion!

Home healthcare providers cared for Sue, becoming very close to her. Sue's condition took a change for the worse. She became difficult, cried often and refused routine treatment. The caregivers became increasingly discouraged and challenged the doctor's orders and treatment of their friend. When Sue died, the caregivers were in an emotional turmoil feeling relief, anger and guilt. Their ambivalence was normal for this situation.

Denial methods serve as protective psychological mechanisms, when people would otherwise be overwhelmed by the reality of death and dying. A mother who has just lost her son through a brain hemorrhage is engulfed by feelings of all kinds. No mother can be expected to cope immediately with the full gamut and extent of the affective states which assail her under such circumstances. Denial — even as a conscious mechanism

— enables her to get some kind of control over the torrent of feelings. People use it to keep experiences, feelings and memories hidden in their subconscious and out of their immediate awareness.[18] It is done all the time.

A teacher, for example, meets with an irate parent not really listening to her or his anger about the principal while she busily continues to complete the necessary papers to transfer the overactive student to another school. Nurses often tell family members that their relative, who just had a serious heart attack and who is barely breathing and clinging to life on an artificial life support machine, is going to be all right. In such instances their own discomfort in dealing with the implications of what bad news might do to the family is evident.

Both adaptive and maladaptive modes of handling such situations can be present within persons at the same time.[19] Along with diverse attitudes, depending on the individual and his/her coping mechanisms, a large number of responses is possible. We react in a variety of ways to the fact of death,[20] and caregivers are no different in this respect from anyone else.

There are many defense mechanisms that people use in the denial process. Defense mechanisms have two characteristics in common: (1) they deny, falsify, or distort reality, and (2) they operate unconsciously so that the person is unaware of what is occurring. [21] Pastor John developed an anxiety about making sure the pastoral care staff had done everything possible after a death at his church. He questioned everyone to find out if they had given the best care to the parishioner. He wanted to make sure that the highest quality care was dispensed. After he talked about his feelings, he discovered some unresolved anxiety about his own father's death. He felt guilty, blaming himself for not doing enough for his father before he died, so he transferred this guilt onto the staff.

Sometimes men and women push themselves over and against the idea of their own mortality, getting rid of thoughts or actions that remind them of death. Strong reactions indicate a fear of death. Sensitive caregivers in such situations provide necessary medical and clinical information and give the patient and family members an opportunity to vent their feelings.

For example the medical staff tried to get a woman to accept her husband's inevitable death and decide to turn off the respirator. The technology delayed the dying process a few days without adding to his quality of life. As the patient's condition continued to worsen the situation caused quite a lot of pain.

Filled with uncertainty and fear, the patient's wife was having difficulty accepting her husband's impending death. I sat with her for an hour and let her express her pain and grief. She gradually became ready to accept the fact that her husband was not going to get better. Her feelings changed from the confusion and torment of a heavy-heart, to a somber acceptance. She began to let go and was ready to have the respirator turned off. She released her husband and at the same time freed herself.

Death remains, even though we may push it aside and refuse to look at it personally, professionally, socially or culturally. We can structure our lives so we don't have to think about death or feel it, at least temporarily. But mortality is always part of our unseen reality.

Many women challenge this "male-dominated" approach to death that so permeates our culture and our consciousness and offer a different approach based on life experience. The question for men at death is the end of life; the question for women is the end of relationships.[22] Many women opt for a more proactive life-centered way of being and seeing.[23] More of us are choosing such an approach, consciously connecting death to life and viewing it as part of living.

Whatever your focus is, here is a reflection for your perusal. Today the cemetery is usually located outside the city's limits — an attempt to deny the reality of death. Only when our cities expand — bringing daily life closer to the location of the cemetery — does one deal with death on a daily basis. Death is not celebrated by our culture as an integral aspect of our living.

Rather it tries to keep death from people's view. The elderly die separated from others in nursing and convalescent homes. Hospitals help to sanitize death, keeping it at arm's length from people's consciousness.[24] And, ironically, most of the healthcare budget in our nation is spent on the last two weeks of life.

I am grateful for the Hospice movement because it attempts to bring death back into the living process as integral to the whole of one's life. Like Hospice, the mission system of a past era included a healthy picture of life that paid attention to living with the reality of death. Throughout the Southwest and Mexico, missions were established that point a finger at our society which suppresses the thought of death. The missions were developed to take in all of life from birth to death — from womb to tomb. Within the walls of the mission, babies were baptized, crops were harvested, inter-generations lived, died and were buried in the mission cemetery — all within the walls, the confines of the community. Birth and the cemetery was a part of one's existence, not pushed aside and hidden. Ancestors were present in daily life, and death was a reality to be remembered.[25]

Denial and Our Creatureliness

In the process of surrendering to new ways of seeing ourselves, we learn the limits of who we are. We must learn to accept that we are not in charge of everything, and we do not have to prove how great we are. We must deal with the griefs and imperfections of being human. When people admit they are looking for the supreme self-transcending power and mystery beyond any self-justification,[26] meaning is open to understanding. Ultimate meaning is discovered when God is seen in all of life.

Life and death engage every aspect of a person's life. It is a sign of maturity when an individual accepts this ongoing developmental process and resigns himself to the process of aging. Such a person accepts his/her true age and stops chasing after his fleeting youth by pretending there is no end to life.[27] Life in this world does end. It must be let go of in very unique and personal ways by everyone.

Unfortunately, there is no provision in a secular world-view for the mourning of one's creatureliness based on some larger design in which to resign oneself securely.[28] And still we know it to be necessary. In accepting the loss of our youth, we begin the process of mourning our own eventual death, bringing it out from the depths of our unconscious where it blocks emotional maturity.[29] To mourn our creatureliness, our mortality, is to move in the direction of personal growth.[30] When this mourning is dealt with we come to grips with our identity before God. This acceptance engages our whole person[31] affecting every aspect of who we are — spiritually, emotionally, physically and socially.

This presupposes that we have an understanding of humankind that embraces human weakness and suffering as a natural, if not necessary, aspect of life, and an understanding of God as the author of life in Whom all loss and grief find meaning.

Implications of Death Anxiety

There are disconcerting signs and growing trends in a society that denies death. One of these is the fact that the majority of people die in institutions rather than at home. Thankfully, this trend is beginning to change with the growth of Hospice and death education programs in schools, hospitals, churches and the media. More people now are dying at home with family and friends. Several studies lend support to this trend citing the fact that those who die in institutions are often isolated from others and sometimes neglected by an overworked and occasionally indifferent hospital staff.

B.G. Glaser and A.L. Strauss in 1966 observed patterns of interaction in six San Francisco area hospitals where they studied the inter-relationships between hospital staff, patients and families. The researchers focused in part on the communications which surround the dying person. The general impression conveyed by this work is that dying individuals often arouse strong fears and a sense of repugnance in those who are charged with their care.[32]

Caregivers find ways to avoid dealing with the dying. Obviously, since family members are often uncomfortable with their loved one's dying, they hope that keeping the patient at the hospital under professional nursing care will relieve them of doing some of the death watch. Nurses may try to pass the task of sitting with the patient off to a family member, or perhaps a chaplain. If no one is around, the nurse may stay away from the patient unless she/he is doing a medical check.[33]

Needless to say, the emotions of the caregivers impact for better or for worse the emotional welfare of the patient facing a life-threatening illness. Caregivers must be aware of and deal with their own feelings about death before they can be effective in helping the dying. Without self-awareness, caregivers and persons in helping roles are vulnerable to a variety of negative feelings and aversive behaviors.[34]

We learn to deal with our anxieties about death in various ways, both healthy and unhealthy. The ways of addressing this issue are linked to our ability to grieve and to bereave the losses of life and especially the loss of our earthly existence in death.

Grief/Bereavement Ministry and Mortality

One Saturday morning in late June, 1991 in San Anselmo, California, I was driving east on one street — having the right of way — when two cyclists turned left in front of my car which was coming right at them. The cyclists did not even flinch. A couple more feet and my moving vehicle would have hit them. A little later when I was driving north on Sir Francis Drake Boulevard, another cyclist pulled in front of my car and then through the oncoming traffic to my left, I almost hit the cyclist three times. Most of us can recall similar incidents where cyclists were almost hit by automobiles. Most of the cyclists were young men oblivious and unmoved by the impending danger around them. They acted as if they were not mortal beings but men impervious to the possibility of death.

Bereavement ministers come face-to-face with human mortality every day and their task is to offer support and comfort to the dying and their loved ones. Through their individual spiritual values, they help them to place their present sufferings in a religious perspective and show them how, with God's help, they can find the courage to accept the inevitable — the end of one's life on earth — and the anxiety of being mortal.[35]

A faith perspective that respects the personal beliefs and values of those who are grieving is basic to this ministry. The pastoral care provider is present to others in their grief as a sign and symbol of the providence of God who is always there in all human suffering and sorrow.[36] They open doors for those in their care helping them to cope by encouraging them to make use of the spiritual resources and potential at their disposal through prayer. Pastoral persons try to encourage people to face death with an attitude of optimism and hope. Christians believe that at death, life is changed not ended; that when our bodies lie in death, we gain everlasting life in Heaven. People are empowered to die well when they are supported by a loving and compassionate circle of caregivers. Concluding any unfinished life issues with loved ones, grieving one's impending death, reaching inner acceptance, living with a belief in a merciful and loving God in a purposeful universe and experiencing a dignity in their dying process,[37] all empower one to die well.

Dying is a process involving considerable emotional ups and downs for everyone. Life is no longer ordered in the way it used to be. The constants are gone, priorities have to be rearranged. Some things have to be held on to, others must be let go. Old habits may have to change and plans for the future may have to be put on hold. The family attempts to stay connected to the dying person taking care of their loved one's wants, needs and requests.[38] It is at such a time that the well-known prayer written by Reinhold Niebuhr can come to mean so much: "Lord, grant me the serenity to accept the things I cannot change, the courage to change the things I can, and the wisdom to know the difference."

Working with family and clients challenges caregivers to draw upon their own life experience and values, their own humanity and spiritual identity to offer helpful interventions that are effective and human. A mixture of possible interventions during the death and dying process include client reaction, family reaction, medical and pastoral interventions.[39] Part of the process of this closure resolves itself in preparing and planning the funeral arrangements.

Christians believe that the Incarnation of Jesus connects our human experiences with that of Christ. Jesus is present to us on our life journey in our pains and joys. Along with helping the dying, the grieving and the bereaved, the caregiver attempts to be with survivors as Jesus is with them. Jesus' presence is one of incarnate love, and the pastoral grief minister manifests this presence through his/her prayer, touch, silence, words, feelings, choices, thoughts, actions and whole being. We are and always hope to be a channel of Christ's presence to the grieving.

The grief-stricken sense His real presence when we stand by them in their pain and help them find meaning in their time of darkness. The pastoral care minister represents the healing community. Through the human companionship of the spiritual health care provider, grieving persons experience the compassionate presence of God and a connection with the community.

A Ministry of Caring

Our care must go beyond the technical and therapeutic dimensions of our skills. It addresses the human spirit giving transcendent hope to those who are suffering: a hope in God's care.[40] Our ministry is a reflection of Jesus' ministry to the sick (cf. Mt 25:36), to the total human person, to the lowly and the poor, the sick and dying.[41]

As caring ministers, we reach out to touch today's lepers, as Jesus did when He walked the shores of Galilee. We serve others in the name of Jesus confronting suffering and offering God's presence to those we meet.[42] We must be equipped to provide help in dealing with those existential (spiritual) concerns which arise in times of illness and dying.[43] The pastoral care minister serves as an emotional/psychological counselor, an ethical adviser and a spiritual guide. The minister of care considers and integrates the physical and social needs of the client into his/her pastoral practice.[44] It is truly a ministry of presence.

Spiritual ministers of care build trust on a foundation of behavior, not on words.[45] We honor this trust when we keep promises, maintain contact, and are available to help others in an empathetic, non-judgmental and confidential manner.[46]

As we provide the security in which individuals feel free to grieve without fear of abandonment or condemnation,[47] we allow them to express their "reality" — however it may surface. This is integral to setting up a safe place to talk about their issues. Obviously some pastoral ministers have attitudes which do not promote this sense of safety in their manner and actions. A judgmental attitude inhibits healing. A caring pastoral relationship can only happen when it is built on mutual trust and respect.

The ministry of caring can help restore and reintegrate persons into the community. In this restoration of self people often become "weller than well," healthier than they were before.[48] When true healing happens, transformation can take place.

When a pastoral person is committed to be with them, the ill and the dying find the quality of their life enhanced. As pastoral care providers, counselors and caring personnel we stand with the sick in their pain and anguish. We enter the emotional tornado of their suffering. We touch the pain. The pastoral care provider is a sign of an ever-present God who never deserts His people in the midst of their emotional storm.

Religious platitudes — pat theological answers from the Bible or one's denominational stance — are not offered to people in order to avoid "getting involved." Rather the caregiver listens to their anguish and pleas, making them aware that God suffers with us in our grief.

Suffering is part of the finite human condition. The isolation that suffering creates can be transformed by the assurance that the God who hung on the cross suffers with us. It is God who enables us to suffer with one another.[49]

An Acceptance of Our Struggles

At one point I resisted continued work on this research project. I could not seem to get the energy to continue to write. When I stopped to look at my reasons I discovered that I did not want to face my own physical vulnerabilities. An injury which I had sustained in an automobile accident years ago was causing low back pain frequently. In writing *Dealing With Grief, Theirs and Ours*, I was personally grieving about the loss of some movement and the physical limitations of my own back.

I was confronted with my own aging, dying process. I thus had attempted to ignore it with no success. As I allowed myself to feel the sadness and to accept my own physical imperfection, I gave myself permission to grieve. I accepted the reality that I would no longer jog or lift weights again, both activities I enjoyed in my earlier years. I let go of a youthful physical image of self. Sadness welled up inside of me as I discarded some assumptions about my physical abilities. Conscious of pain associated with ordinary undertakings like walking around, sitting for an extended period, engaging in some simple stretching exercises or even lying prostrate on my bed to go to sleep, I was reminded of my own mortality.

Once I started to face these physical limitations squarely, I became aware of how they pointed to another deeper reality in my life. Reading some of the materials on grief, they awakened in me some old and new anxieties about my own death. I had some concerns that I would not be able to finish some personal goals I wanted to complete. As I let go, though, I found that the realization of the inevitability of my death became clearer, more tangible and, yes, even acceptable. And there were gifts associated with this acceptance.

My energy was no longer blocked. I was able to continue my writing, studying and reflection on this subject. I was able to move from resistance to the thought of my own dying to an acceptance marked with a new freedom — a kind of resurrection. I was once again eager to enter once more into the fullness of my own life journey with all its ups and downs. I embraced life.

By accepting our own human vulnerabilities, we are able to enter into the struggles of others. By honestly recognizing our own frailties and powerlessness, we prepare ourselves to meet others in their losses and grief — to become wounded healers like our Lord.

Chapter Two

THE EXPERIENCE OF LOSS, GRIEF AND RECOVERY

The Experience of Loss

Loss is defined as no longer possessing, or doing without something or someone, which was important and valued. Loss is applied to a separation, a severance preceding the loss, a temporary loss and the fear of loss. These experiences: loss, separation and fear of loss are universal to all people at every stage of the life cycle.[1] Therefore loss is integral to the diversity of human experience. Some losses may be obvious like death; others, such as unfulfilled expectations, are not always recognized as such.[2]

A major scientific study of the survivors and victims of the Cocoanut Grove nightclub fire in which nearly 500 people were killed in Boston in 1942 was conducted by Erich Lindemann.[3] The survivors experienced the kind of grief that is a normal and necessary reaction to loss. The focus, though, of a lot of the studies which followed was on how people cope in a crisis, rather than on how they grieve.[4]

It is easier to encourage a person to cope with loss than to help them face the pain. By using coping techniques, professionals can find ways to circumvent their own feelings in such instances. Therapists, social workers, clergy, nursing personnel and others may too readily diagnose the common symptoms of grief as a psychiatric disorder. But true healing can not take place without the journey through the grieving process.

Professional caregivers have to be aware of their own personal losses if they are to care competently and with empathy for the sufferings of others. Those who are blind to their own losses will not clearly identify their clients' problems, nor will they be able to relate to them.[5]

The inability to identify loss sets the stage for a lack of fully resolving one's grief. This avoidance carries with it resulting health problems. Unresolved grief issues leave a residue setting the stage for future difficulties. Incomplete grieving is the forerunner of a wide range of physical, emotional and mental disorders.[6] In the work of one researcher, loss is correlated to other emotional disorders. This research points to a direct connection between the sudden loss of a loved one and chronic loneliness as a factor in premature death.[7]

Severe losses in children can have lasting effects on their lives for years to come. Some children may become adults who have difficulty developing ties of intimacy because of earlier traumatic experiences — like losing their parents. They may have difficulty finishing projects, fear accomplishment and doing well, find times of separation unduly painful, have mental problems and a tendency to act in harmful ways.[8]

Loss and insufficient grieving will find their way into one's daily life and pattern of relating. People depend on previously learned coping styles to deal with their current losses. Certain variables, an inability to manage their affairs, life changes and stressors affect one's and one's family's ability to deal with loss. Caregivers facilitate a movement toward effective collaboration among people in their life decisions even when the grieving process is skewed due to dysfunctional family dynamics.

In one situation I walked into a hospital room of a dying 25-year-old woman who was in an irreversible persistent vegetative state. In the room were her widowed father, three other sisters and a brother. The family dynamics were dysfunctional.

The two oldest girls competed for the matriarchal role of the mother who had died when these two were teenagers. The youngest daughter acted as a peacemaker trying to settle the fights between her older sisters. The father was a workaholic who passively succumbed to his oldest daughters. The son, the third oldest sibling, who lived out of state arrived the following day — acting somewhat uninvolved and passive.

I noticed how the two oldest daughters vied for control of the family and their father's affection. They always seemed to be angry with each other. Each tried to get their peacemaker sister to join with her against her rival sister. The son, who was in treatment for clinical depression, complained about being misunderstood and unappreciated. He would disappear for hours on end without letting any of the family know where he was.

The father had long since relinquished a lot of his influence over his children by not owning his feelings and authority. I discovered that after the mother's death the two oldest daughters ran the household, taking charge of the family. Conflict, anger, guilt, hostility, triangulation, yelling and unhealthy ways of behaving towards one another characterized their relationships with each other for years. It took two weeks of intense work with them before they were able to come together and resolve their issues for the moment, giving their daughter/sister some kind of peace. A week later the young woman died.

Our ways of relating with others emerge as sign posts in times of loss. They are the telltale symptoms at times of loss gone bad. By helping people deal more effectively with loss and grief, the pastoral caregiver can be instrumental in enabling grieving persons to move on to more creative living.[9] To do so, they must be aware that earlier losses often pre-condition people to how they will experience later losses, including the loss associated with their own death.[10]

Types of Loss

Loss manifests itself in an assortment of forms or combinations meshing together.

Relationship loss is the loss of a significant loved or valued person, the cessation of opportunities to dialogue, share experiences with and be in the presence of that person.[11]

Functional loss is the loss of a particular bodily function. It also includes the deprivation of a degree of independence resulting from the partial or full loss of the use of a part of one's physical organs, appendages or sight.[12]

Structural loss is when a person actually loses part of his/her body. Examples of structural losses include limb amputation, mastectomy, colostomy, loss of kidneys, loss of hair or teeth, etc.[13]

Intrapsychic loss occurs when someone loses some inner sense or image of self.[14] This happens when a person discards some vision or goal which is not realistic (e.g., of starting his/her own company and making a lot of money).

Material loss is the losing of a physical object or a particular surrounding to which one has an important bond[15] like a home, a car or a certain piece of jewelry.

Social loss is the loss of role, reputation, cultural and family patterns.[16] We experience social loss when we take on new social roles[17] through divorce or a new career at mid-life.

Systemic loss recalls that human beings usually belong to some interactional system in which patterns of behavior develop over time. Examples are when a young adult leaves his/her family of origin,[18] when a priest leaves his religious order; or when a career officer leaves the military.

Developmental losses are part of change and growth. These losses include the developmental process from conception, through birth, to death. Even birth itself is a separation trauma.[19]

Changes take place in a dynamic way as we travel the paths of life through the developmental phases. We have changes that take place along the path of life either with or without our awareness:

I've Got the Time

When I was a boy of thirteen,
All of life stretched out before me,
Life was like a carnival —
there was popcorn, ice cream in a cone,
ferris wheel rides, bumper cars, candied apples,
men on tightropes, women dangling from a trapeze bar.
Oh, look at my possibilities,
so much to see and so much to do,
I'll do it all, I've got the time.
When I became a young man of twenty-one,
I could reach the moon.
All the earth was my playground,
with circus animals, stunts, and fantasies around.
Race cars, hot air balloons, river rafting, marathons,
tackle football games, power weight lifting.
Oh, see the possibilities,
so much to see and so much to do,
I'll do it all, I've got the time.
As the clock turned,
time moves on.
Tomorrow has come,
now I'm a mid-lifer,
content at short walks, sitting at my computer,
pacing myself.
Journeys have ends,
time is letting me know it's in charge.
Less seeing and doing.
I won't see it all and do it all.
Enjoying who I am,

Enjoying this moment.
Life moves on, I move on,
We both change with time,
that's alright.
My time is changing,
My time is shorter,
slipping away with each day (Roussell, Jr., '96).[20]

Within the shortening of our lives, within the mystery of loss and gain, we come to integrate a personal sense of the Incarnation in our own journey. I come face to face with the reality of the Cross and Resurrection as I experience personal loss and gain. How I appropriate the losses and gains reflects the quality of acceptance of Cross and Resurrection in my life. This is an area of further study that I will address later in the theological discourse of Chapter Three.

Loss and Illness

How I deal with what comes my way in life, plays a large role in my predisposition for health or illness. Yet there are some life circumstances that by their very nature seem to be predictors for the onset of disease. Dr. Harold G. Wolff and his colleague, Dr. Thomas Holmes, of the University of Washington School of Medicine, did a study of patients who had colds and nasal infections. When patients came in for medical care, the doctors asked them to come back when they had recovered. When each patient returned, blood flow, freedom of breathing, swelling and secretion in the nose were measured. The patient was asked about the event or events that had occurred before he or she became ill. After a conversation about a mother-in-law, for instance, or retirement, the measurements were repeated. Discussion of the event renewed the old symptoms. In fact, so many patients mentioned mother-in-law visits, that Wolff and

Homes began to consider them a common cause of disease in the United States.[21]

One study revealed that life events clustered in a two-year period before the onset of tuberculosis, heart disease, skin disease and hernia.[22] Researchers set up a scale to guide them in predicting the onset of disease. In all, 394 persons were asked to rate the amount of social readjustment required for each of the forty-three changes in life patterns.[23] The event requiring the greatest amount of social readjustment was the death of a spouse, which was then assigned a mean value of 100. All other life events were assigned mean values relative to the loss of a spouse.[24]

The life events themselves, the way an individual views these events, changes and losses; and their patterns of coping, thinking and styles of behavior are all part of the multi-faceted causes for the development of a disease.[25] Medical researchers agree that there is an important relationship between mind and body. However, they question any simple hypothesis that attitude changes alone are the key to health and propose more scientific study to develop a complex understanding of the interrelationships.[26]

Losses in Later Life

We grieve losses that are really temporary "attachments." We grieve for our waning health, the loss of a job and the death of family and friends. We know that none of these things will last forever, yet, we still cherish and grieve for them. With this realization we are challenged not to make any of these attachments into "little gods."[27] We experience a sense of freedom in defining their real importance in the broader scale of things.[28] The longer one lives, the number of losses increases. This life pattern — one loss piling on another — complicates the grief process.[29]

People who accept the fact that they are aging fare better

as they grow older. People must be able to accept life in its entirety. Part of this means accepting who and what we are at each and every stage of life. There is peace in acknowledging that we are no longer as young as we once were. A married person who accepts his or her identity as a spouse and no longer a single person is much happier than one who continues to try passing as someone unattached. When people pretend to be what they are not — they are living a lie and experience all the uneasiness, discomfort and disharmony that normally accompanies such a stance. When we embrace the truth about where we are in life, we become more authentic and real in all that we do. We become who we really are.[30] In aging well, a person develops the ability to let go of emotional investments that are gone and to reinvest in new attachments.[31]

In recognizing that our health is changing in the aging process, and that our assumptions and ground rules about life have to change, we — along with the whole of creation — are in "bondage to decay." By discarding ways of thinking and attachments which ignore this fact, we can change our thinking and make adjustments in the way we live — in our lifestyles, "groaning within ourselves as we wait for... the redemption of our bodies" (Rm 8:21-23).[32]

We need to develop a spirituality that does not equate our persons with our bodies as we grow older. Our true being and essence is not limited to our physical body.[33] As human beings, we are composed of body, mind, soul and spirit together in one unified whole.

As we age we become more aware of discomfort, pain, and other physical difficulties. But there is a value in learning, with the grace of God, to transcend our physical sufferings and even to rise above them.[34] Much of our healthcare environment operates from the opposite perspective focusing on the physical and ignoring the transcendental dimensions of life. Modern healthcare tends to keep people alive physically no matter the burdens and costs. The cases of Karen Ann Quinlan and Nancy Cruzan demonstrate healthcare's overemphasis on the physical dimensions of healing. Both of these individuals were in irreversible comas for years, being kept alive by a mechanical ventilator. Only after family members petitioned the courts were artificial life supports removed.[35]

As we grow older we need to adopt a more spiritual way of viewing losses. As this happens, we accept the stripping away of who we have been, and in this "kenosis" or emptying of self we discover our true spiritual identity.[36] When most of our other identities are lost, a spiritual identity can and should help us to transcend the losses of this life.[37]

A number of years ago the importance of one's spiritual identity hit home for me. I remember a woman who had been brought into the Emergency Room at the hospital after being hit by a car. She was walking across the street when a car came from out of nowhere and struck her. She was thrown to the side of the street, and the driver kept on going, speeding away from the scene of the accident. Shortly after the woman arrived at the hospital, her husband came in and joined the staff in the trauma room. She was awake but not able to talk. The physician motioned for the woman's husband, who was standing next to his wife, to come outside the room so he could talk to him about her condition. He told the husband that she had some internal bleeding but it didn't look serious, and a broken leg. She had a lot of bruises on her face and elsewhere because of the accident. She would have to undergo surgery to take care of the internal bleeding and her leg.

After surgery the woman was brought to a room where her husband sat waiting for her. The surgeon came up to the room to talk about her condition. He told the husband there would be no permanent damage from the accident. The woman was covered in bandages and gauze, she had one leg in a cast, and she was still sedated. As the doctor finished he said, "I know she doesn't look the same as you are used to, being covered in all these bandages. She'll look this way for a few weeks until she heals." Then the husband, who was smiling at his sleeping wife with a look of love and tenderness and touching her right hand, without turning his gaze from his wife, responded to the physician, "She looks pretty good to me!"

Through the gauze, medical accouterments, facial bruising, this husband saw his wife's true identity. She was beautiful in his eyes no matter how she appeared. He saw through to who she was, a child of God — his dearest wife and friend. He saw her true spiritual person beyond the way she appeared. I was struck by his love and ability to let go of what was superficial, extraneous and untrue about his wife. His love saw past the physical to her spiritual being and essence.

In seeing people for who they are spiritually, we surrender all superficial attachments and center on that person's spiritual core. The spiritual and emotional healthcare provider who is able to shed his or her unauthentic attachments (including unrealistic personal expectations, assumptions, etc.) is bound to be more effective in his or her guidance of a client who is still struggling with life's attachments.

Attachment

All attachments build on the most primal connection between the mother and her infant. Later losses are based on the loss of this mother-child connection.[38] The attachment process is a very natural process for human beings. Separation from an attachment is painful. Depending on the degree of investment, there will be a greater or lesser level of personal grief when our attachments are lost or no longer with us.[39] For some persons a significant loss can take on a significance that goes beyond ordinary grief. The loss is viewed as a threat to all significant attachments including an individual's own life.[40] To advance to a state of wholeness in life, these lost attachments must be grieved while being firmly rooted in a Presence beyond oneself.

Grief

In *Macbeth*, William Shakespeare gives voice to the fact that failure to mourn is hazardous to one's health. "Give sorrow words; the grief that does not speak, whispers the o'er fraught heart and bids it break."[41]

The mourning process is a normative reality that touches the whole person. A complete assessment of the grief process necessitates the development of a comprehensive model and (w)holistic approach encompassing physical, behavioral, emotional, cognitive and spiritual integration.[42]

A person uses left-brain control strategies to get through the grieving process, holding on to his/her understanding of self and his/her identity. If taken to an extreme a person's tight grip can become rigid and compulsive.[43] To get through our grieving, we discard assumptions and behaviors that seem no longer useful to us. We separate, let go and withdraw from our past. When taken to an extreme, these letting go strategies can engender loneliness and anti-social behavior.[44] One widow, for example, never left her home. She destroyed all pictures, artifacts and anything that represented memories of her past. Sometimes people use a mixture of 'holding on' and 'letting go' strategies. Coping with loss through combinations of both strategies creates a tension that swings back and forth with an ambiguous quality.[45] Others use combinations of both creating a sense of balance.

A comprehensive grief model entails the following phases: an initial awareness, an awareness of the extent of the loss, gaining perspective, resolving loss, reformulating loss and transforming loss.[46]

In the beginning phase an individual experiences *shock* making use of either holding on or letting go strategies.[47] In this phase, the body marshals the individual for "flight or fight." Different people experience a variety of feelings. Some, for example search for spiritual meaning and purpose in their lives.[48]

In the next phase people *mourn*. They experience aches and pains, loss of energy and appear to be distant. Their thoughts center on the consequences of their loss. They confront their own human existence and eventual death.[49]

Gradually the person's pain and the intensity of the feelings diminish and they may develop a new consciousness that is more open, calm and pardoning.[50]

In time, the griever shares with others an acknowledgment of the loss with its implications for a different life. As the grieving process continues people have a deeper sense of responsibility and appreciation for life.[51]

Here the bereaved continues on this healing path toward a more cosmic and integrative perspective. People become conscious that everything is temporary and they begin to focus on living more fully and being open to the possibility of wonder and surprise.[52]

Now more open to life's possibilities, they can move into the final transformation phase. Here there is a new depth of self-appreciation joined with energies for loving, creating and venturing. There is sense of connection to everyone and everything, and all of life is experienced as a gift. At this point the person experiences an integration of their intellectual (cognitive), physical, behavioral, emotional and spiritual energies. Unlike in earlier phases, there are no boundaries between these energies.[53]

When people reach this phase, they can experience God as present and fundamental to the entire integration process. God is present as the source and goal of their transformation. This phase is a kind of Resurrection experience that is integrated into the ordinary extraordinariness of life. Spiritual and emotional caregivers encourage and even accelerate this process through their joyful, empathetic, forgiving, open and inclusive service to those who journey through the mystery of grief. We become the conduit to energies which are within and beyond ourselves.

Anticipatory Grief

Anticipatory grief is a dry run of what is to come. Beginning the grief process, people become aware of their own mortality or the potential death of someone else. Anticipatory grief is real grief triggered by the possibility of one's own, or of a loved one's death. Family, friends and others go through anticipatory grief preceding a person's death. But this does not exempt them from further suffering. After the person dies, the survivors still go through the ordinary grief process, in spite of their preliminary grieving for their loved one.[54]

Generally — although usually not recognized — anticipatory grief encompasses all the processes of mourning, coping, interaction, planning and psychosocial reorganization begun through a person's response to an impending loss. Those experiencing anticipatory grief struggle with a delicate balance among the mutually conflicting demands of simultaneously holding onto, letting go of, and drawing closer to dying. In the process[55] — whether of one's own death or the passing of another — anticipatory grief deals with the whole person with their past, present and future, as well as with their unique tensions and styles of coping. It involves psychological, social, physiological, intellectual and spiritual factors.

In this interim phase a whole continuum of feelings — depression, heightened preoccupation with the deceased, thoughts on functioning without the departed — all aspects and phases of anticipatory grief[56] and involving every dimension of the person, come to the fore as people recognize a myriad of issues and emotions rising to consciousness. Some people have feelings of guilt and anxiety over having too little time to settle issues and put things in order with their loved one. Still others do not seem to go through these stages; rather they accept the person's death and move toward resolution regarding their impending loss.

Persons must confront a multiplicity of issues in the living-dying interval[57] between diagnosis and death. The dying person needs: to take care of legal arrangements (making out a will and funeral arrangements); to deal with the idea of his or her death and separation from loved ones; to plan his or her care, choosing how he or she wants to spend the time that remains; and to confront emotional issues that may arise.[58] Through resolving and completing these tasks people care for themselves. Caregivers assist them in reassessing their inner resources in contemplation of God. We help people understand and experience the power of the Resurrection in the events that cause this phase of grief.[59]

Abnormal Grief

When grief does not move toward healing, a person begins to be carried along a path toward abnormal grief reactions.[60] If abnormal grief is intensified through maladaptive behavior, it needs to be resolved through the mourning process.

People in ambivalent relationships — with excessive amounts of anger and guilt — have difficulty grieving normally. People who experience multiple losses may be hampered in their grieving process. Early childhood losses and personality factors, like withdrawing socially, hinder grieving. Some losses have a social taboo and must be kept secret. The survivor finds little compassion from the community in working through such losses.[61]

When people do not finish the grieving process, the stage is set for abnormal and complicated grief expressions. *Chronic grief reactions* are extreme, disproportionate, and sustained. They are postponed, not reaching an adequate resolution. *Delayed reactions* are deferred or restrained with subdued emotional reaction. When triggered by some later loss the person grieves at an excessive level that is not necessary for this future situation. Another group of reactions are *exaggerated,* extreme and restricting. People have an aversion to death. They have a persistent sense of despair and hopelessness. *Masked grief reactions* are dulled exhibiting unnatural, irregular or strange behavior and may include psychotic symptoms of acting out.[62]

In *The Rosary Murders*[63] we are provided with an extreme example of masked grief. In this film, a teenage girl is murdered by her father who keeps her room exactly the same for years. He turns it into a ritual mausoleum, never changing anything in it. By leaving the room untouched, he never confronts the crime or deals with his abnormal grieving.

However, there are exceptions in which some individuals exhibit the symptoms of complicated grief, but are working through the grief in their unique personal or cultural way. In making choices about their support networks and social relationships, their values and personal emotional resources,[64] people work through and complete their grief process. They move on to recovery and rediscover new meaning in their lives.

Recovery and Meaning

As we recover from grief, healing takes place. We find restoration and a sense of meaning as we ask ourselves two questions: How and Why? The 'how' seeks an understanding of the sequence of events that led up to the loss. The 'why' represents our search for meaning. These questions lie at the core of our human existential probing and search for meaning.[65] We attempt to master the storms of life by finding palatable reasons for our personal suffering. With the discovery of meaning comes the possibility of restoration.

Restoration implies that we have come to terms with the mystery of life and death in every dimension of our persons. Although many of these questions cannot be fully answered to our satisfaction here on earth, we discover that there is an overarching meaning behind it all and arrive at an integration that accepts our life-experience as part of the reality of a greater mystery. When we face all human experience, the living and the dying, with a willingness to engage mystery, then we are able to contemplate all of the questions, concerns and the affirmations of what it is to be human. This contemplation will lead us to see that life ultimately affirms us daily and in an ongoing way. We accept our existence as something being daily affirmed in the midst of our ups and downs by a Presence beyond.

Reflecting on the condition of her terminally ill father, one woman said, "I feel so powerless and deficient." By pressing him to eat, making him walk around the nursing home and insisting that he have a will to keep on trying no matter how he felt, revealed her desperation to maintain his life. She was forcing him to stay alive when he no longer wanted to do so. The older man was angry at her attempts. He was ready to die and meet his Maker. She found it difficult to let him die since she was an only child, and her mother had passed away years before. It became the challenge of the pastoral caregiver to help the woman understand her father's need to let go. When she was finally able to hear his wishes and to release him, he was able to die peacefully. He knew he was affirmed by God, by Existence, and was prepared and ready to die.

Each person's life is special by the mere fact that he or she exists. Life at its core expresses a deeper more fundamental spiritual perception experienced even in times of mourning. In the Beatitudes Jesus acknowledges the blessedness of those who in their mourning operate through a faith perspective. They have a strength and comfort which are basic and solid — taking on an eternal dimension.[66] Religion assists in one's recovery by affirming life. Such a base provides perspective for those times when life-events may distort our view of things. This strengthens faith and courage and makes grace available. Then the promised blessedness is discovered in the very process of wise mourning.[67]

Recovery takes place when we learn to live with the fact of adversity and are not destroyed by it. When we focus our attention on the indestructible values of ultimate meaning and Divine potential, grief and suffering become an opportunity for growth and personal integrity. As we focus on the Eternal/Divine source of life, we learn to live with grief.[68]

Obviously, not everyone who recovers from grief has an integrating spiritual experience. We recover from grief in a multitude of ways. Some get through the recovery process by hard work or by occupying themselves with personal interests and satisfying tasks. The caregiver's challenge is to be comfortable in allowing people to recover in whatever way works best for them. Many others, though, move through grief towards greater wholeness in and through the values of a creative faith and hope, and come to live a fuller, more abundant life. Through the eyes of faith they experience the amazing grace of continual affirmation. By accepting the promises of Resurrection and rebirth and cooperating with the grace of God, they experience ever-recurring opportunities in life itself to move beyond loss and failure, and to grow through trial and pain toward new perspectives and greater faith.

When we listen anew to our own inner being in times of loss, a clearer vision and understanding of who we are takes place. Entering into the Divine life within and growing in the awareness of the Divine breath of life in and throughout our lives, we create new energy and joy. The more we understand what is going on within, the more we grow in greater consciousness of God's grace taking flesh within us. Through empathetic listening and understanding, we learn to reclaim our spiritual identity and re-center on the privilege of our calling to affirm life in the presence of death.

Chapter Three

BIBLICAL AND THEOLOGICAL RESOURCES: INCARNATION, CROSS AND RESURRECTION

Just as God enters into our personal world, so we who strive to be "empathetic listeners" enter into the world of others with understanding and true respect. In this way empathy is in a sense an expression of incarnational theology.

A theology of Incarnation speaks of God's self-emptying: "Christ Jesus... though he was in the form of God, did not regard equality with God something to be exploited. Instead, he emptied himself and took on the form of a slave, being born in human likeness" (Ph 2:6-7). God's Incarnation as a man made possible the divine total gift of self on the Cross for us. The Cross and Death of Jesus is the ultimate identification of God with humanity.

St. Thérèse of Lisieux, in one of her many letters, talks about the humanity of Christ and the human sacrifices that are sometimes asked of us as they were of him. "Our Lord," she wrote, "never asks us for sacrifices that are beyond our strength. It is true that sometimes this divine Savior makes us taste all the bitterness of the chalice which He presents to our soul. And when He asks the sacrifice of all that is most dear in this world it is impossible, apart from a very special grace, not to cry out as He did Himself in the Garden of His agony: 'Father, let this chalice pass from me... nevertheless, not my will but Yours be done.'"[1]

It was in embracing the Cross, because He recognized in it the will of His Heavenly Father, that peace came to Jesus as it will come to us when we do the same. On the Cross, God shows us the very divine essence of total abandonment and made possible the gift of eternal life for us all. In the Cross, we recognize that God is truly with us — giving meaning to all our suffering. But it doesn't end there.

God the Father accepted and vindicated the life and death of his only-begotten Son in the mystery of the Resurrection — by restoring life. This divine action — this cosmic revelation of the mystery of death and life, Cross and Resurrection — for the Christian, is at the heart of all reality. It gives birth to a theology of hope, celebrating how God vindicates and restores humanity through healing, forgiveness and life. Ultimately our future will be characterized by peace and joy: "He will wipe every tear from their eyes. Death will be no more; no more grief or crying or pain, for what came before has passed away" (Rv 21:4).[2] All will experience the fullness of life without end.

Empathic Understanding

The development of empathic listening is integral to helping others pursue their journey through death to life. An empathic listener learns to enter into the world of another. This kind of presence is an art, the art of being with another in a state of loving listening.[3]

The spiritual and emotional care provider hears the other, understands and responds to how the client sees life. The caregiver sensitively and delicately listens. Like Moses standing on holy ground, the caregiver is called to see God's movement within another's unique frame of reference and experience of the world. Unfortunately spiritual and emotional caregivers do not always act out of this frame of reference. They get stuck in their biases and professional modes of acting that can short-circuit genuine empathy, blur their vision, and impede their mission as caregivers.

Empathic understanding is the ability to see accurately into the client's private world. The therapist views the client's world 'as if' it were his or her own.[4] Sensitive to the other's felt experience without judging it, he or she tries to maintain a safe environment for the client. Respecting the person's process, the caregiver is careful not to expose unconscious threatening feelings.[5] Putting aside their own biases, they communicate what is sensed from the other's world, and continually check the accuracy of their perceptions about the other's views, feelings, thoughts and wants.[6]

Caregivers who are secure in themselves keep centered and can comfortably return to their own world at any time. With a commitment to service as a personal priority, those who desire to serve must learn, over time, how to accept themselves and others,[7] excluding all prejudice and bias that could cause them to fail in their pastoral intention.

Incarnational Theology and Empathy

Empathy can be experienced through the letting go of one's center (dying to self), the holding on to one's center (keeping of self) and combinations of both of these. God enters and confirms human experience letting go of divinity, not ceasing to be fully Divine, and allowing the mystery of both to interact in all human experience.

These two qualities of empathy are expressions of incarnational theology. First, we move into the frame of reference of another while holding on to our own ground and person. Secondly, we enter into the world of another while forgetting for a time our own center/ground. We engage another person by using one or the other, or by combining both.

The Incarnation of God connects both these aspects of empathy. God empties self and takes the form of a slave, being born in human likeness (Ph 2:7). God retains self in the resurrection and final divine exaltation. (Christ, the divine, empties himself to the point of death on the cross, is raised from the dead and exalted above all creation.) This "Paschal Mystery" of God sets up a relationship with humanity which is the core, the central way of being for all life.

An essential element of this mystery has to do with atonement — the restoration of broken relationships.[8] The Bible speaks of the primacy of right relationship over right doing and right knowing. The term "heart" as understood in Scripture expresses this priority of relationship.[9] The biblical meaning of the heart refers to the core of one's being, the center of one's personality, the deepest portion of a person, the most interior choice and desire,[10] the center of consciousness. In this sense the 'heart' of a person is called to be with God, self, and others in right relationship, a right way of being lived out in how one exists with others. This is the central understanding of the eternal covenant — offering *shalom* or peace to all. Over and over the Hebrew and Christian Scriptures express the priority of the pure heart over both "knowing" and "doing" (Mt 5:8).[11]

In pastoral grief counseling, we help people attain insight (teaching right thought) and help them act in healthy, constructive ways (urging right behavior). However, the primacy of quality of life comes before quality of thought or quality of behavior.[12] Before people are assisted in thinking new thoughts and acting in new ways, we must first set up a covenanted relationship with them. This relationship provides space for them to experience restoration, comfort, health, sustenance, guidance, reconciliation and nurturance in their grieving.

A cab driver from a large mid-western city, burdened by feelings that he wasn't good enough and that nobody liked him, came in for pastoral counseling over a period of several months. In his pastoral therapeutic sessions he was given room to learn and love himself. As he talked and grieved over his unrealistic self-image, he began to alter his perceptions of self. Gradually new insights simmered into consciousness, taking shape and affecting a positive change. He became less critical of himself and others. His sullenness gave way to a brighter attitude toward life. He enjoyed his own company and became a friend to himself.

Incarnation

Obviously spiritual and pastoral counselors are not always successful in bringing comfort, health and nurturance to all those in their care. There are insidious "power issues" in the helping professions. Some counselors operate from a position of "power." While desiring to foster the good, these individuals often set their egos above all else, allowing their own unconscious drive for power to suggest the illusion of help. This approach deprives clients of power and self-esteem and ultimately does not bring any real nurturance.[13] Effective spiritual counselors initiate quality and loving relationships by being with people in healthy ways under the guidance of the Holy Spirit. In so doing, their actions and communications are visible expressions of the transcendent forgiveness and love of God.[14]

Like the drive for power, personal issues, preoccupations, fatigue, etc., may block people from fully experiencing God's tangible presence. The spiritual and pastoral caregiver, the nurse, health care provider, chaplain, clergy, teacher and/or lay pastoral care volunteer must constantly remind themselves of the importance of their commitment to be available to others in their need. They incarnate the reality of God in their roles of assistance.

Recently a man came to me confused about his decision to permit his unconscious wife to die naturally. She had a terminal heart disease, and was being kept alive by receiving oxygen and other nutrients. Without a heart transplant, she would only live another few months. Previously she had chosen, with the help of her pastor and family, to abandon all and any burdensome and disproportionate treatment, which would only prolong her inevitable death. She had filled out a healthcare advance directive, giving her husband the authority to speak as her proxy. But the husband was having second thoughts about honoring her decision to end the extra medical treatment. Even though the burden of the treatment outweighed the benefits derived, the children were willing to go along with their father, even against their mother's wishes.

As I listened to his wavering back and forth, I entered into his personal stress and conflict over this decision. Gradually, as his troubled feelings were expressed, he was able to see the medical reality more clearly and what was best for his wife. In coming to the decision to let her die naturally, he was at peace.

The caregiver incarnates a caring presence when helping people to find meaning in the oftentimes seemingly meaningless circumstances of their lives by assisting them in ethical, spiritual and crisis situations.[15]

Our pastoral care reveals how God relates to humanity. The meaning of the Incarnation — God coming into our lives — is a reversal of all worldly values. In Mary's *Magnificat*, all of creation sings, 'God has filled the hungry with good things, and sent the rich away empty' (Luke 1:53).[16] In Jesus' Incarnation, all forms of power over human beings — sexism, racism, elitism — are critiqued by the way of humility.[17] God chooses to join the world of humanity through a concrete expression of humility. All people no matter what creed, gender, economic status and national origin are called by the Incarnation to a life of humility, to a process of conversion. It is a way evidenced by a God with a preferential option for the lowly and all who are victimized in life. The spiritual and emotional care provider acts and listens in ways that do not foster dominance, manipulation or victimization. The professional caregiver develops non-harmful techniques for helping others by acquiring genuine humility.

Unfortunately, we are not always humble. A physician told a man, who was hospitalized for attempted suicide, to 'just get over' his emotional problems. Having said that, the medical 'professional' walked out of the room — an action which demeaned and further victimized the suicidal man's sense of self. Pastoral professionals can act in harmful ways too. After years of being outside of the Christian community, a man made an attempt to come back to church. Just when he found the courage to try to reconnect, a clergy member attacked the man publicly — calling him a heathen. Those who let their personal biases govern, harm those under their charge. The challenge is to be aware of how one's professionalism or viewpoint could get in the way of being a channel for the Divine.

The caregiver who chooses to share in the other's condition, involving himself/herself in their personal history, concretizes God's non-judgmental, unconditional love. In a tangible way he or she is a "living incarnator of divinity."[18] Spiritual, pastoral care and counseling, pastoral grief care and grief/bereavement counseling are rooted in a Christology of the mystery of "God becoming human." In the prologue of John's Gospel (1:14), the starting point of all Christology, the Word of God becoming flesh as human is revealed and proclaimed.

We are challenged to ground our ministry in this Divine mystery without gender or other labels. Feminist theology challenges us to understand God beyond all gender bias.[19] In Christ, God exists as both an historical being and as a trans-historical being. Human events throughout time and history reveal the Divine presence in every person.

Every person has been offered the Divine in Christ and should be helped and encouraged to experience the full value of this gift.[20] Because God has embraced humanity, the task of the caregiver is to help people to celebrate all that is fully human, regardless of gender, race, nationality or class. We work not alone but out of the mystery of the Church, which is the servant of the mystery of Christ. We ultimately depend on Christ for support in this pastoral outreach, as God works through all our human talents and skills. Jesus Christ is the fount and foundation of all that is accomplished in the healing and caring ministry. Ultimately all healing finds its source in God.

Knowing the importance of connecting to this divine wellspring of healing, we must look deeper than the disease or problems which people present to us. As agents of change, we are committed to seeing the inner possibility in every person, for every person carries the incarnate image of God. I believe each of is called to assist others in integrating this authentic vision of personhood. Incarnational images of God embody loving expressions which use power to persuade, not to coerce. Images of God as mother, sister and friend reflect how God works in relational ways through human agents. God's liberating power is manifested in the powerlessness of the Cross in which we clearly see the evil ways that power has been used through the ages.[21]

Helping people get in touch with life's great values within their personal history, culture and religious journey, puts them in touch with the uncreated energies of this uncreated God. The pastoral and spiritual healthcare provider walks with people in this incarnational journey to authentic personal freedom. God manifests divinity throughout all reality including their own situation.

Pope John Paul II develops the universality of God's saving power offered to all in the Incarnate Christ when he writes:

> The universality of salvation means that it is granted not only to those who explicitly believe in Christ and have entered the Church.... But it is clear that today, as in the past, many people do not have an opportunity to come to know or accept the gospel revelation or to enter the Church... for such people salvation in Christ is accessible by virtue of a grace which, while having a mysterious relationship to the Church, does not make them formally part of the Church but enlightens them in a way which is accommodated to their spiritual and material situation. This grace comes from Christ....[22]

Spiritual caregivers walk with people helping integrate their life journey with its knowns and unknowns. Joined to the Incarnate Word — expressed in their personal values and diverse religious experiences — caregivers guide and empower the mystical and mysterious relationship present in all peoples of every culture and religion. Authentic and compassionate care providers make the Gospel real in different and diverse cultures, values, peoples, religions, denominations, spiritualities, ethical norms, philosophies and belief systems.

Together with their prospective religions and value systems, all persons are welcomed into God's community. The goal of caring persons is to transmit their own values through fully entering the other's reality. The connection is made with respect, genuineness, empathy, warmth, positive regard, affirmation and dignity. The client experiences the caregiver fully entering into their experience. A respect of incarnational values challenges caregivers to fully respect the freedom of every person they serve. This respect of human dignity and the reality of grace, evidences how each care provider stands convinced of the inner conscious and unconscious workings of the Spirit. Already existing within people is an expectation, even if an unconscious one, of knowing God and the deepest values and meanings connected with life.[23]

When I began my ministry, I thought I had all the answers. But after years of working as a chaplain, pastoral educator, spiritual guide and pastoral counselor, I now view things differently. God's presence and action in the world is not confined in any way. I have experienced God's presence in women in prison, those who are agnostic, believers of Native and Tribal Religious traditions, practitioners of Buddhism, adherents of Hinduism and Judaism, and in all the denominations of the Christian community. We are challenged to enter the Divine music of another's life picking up the pulse and rhythm that we find there. We sit with people at times with little or no conversation and in the silence, the smiling gestures, understanding flows between us.

As we listen to the other, he or she experiences an awareness of being understood. The language of our spiritual counseling is beyond words as our beings connect in the moment.[24]

A woman, anxious about an upcoming surgery, was in need of acceptance and affirmation as, with tears pouring down her face, she revealed her fears about death, about not being there for her daughter as she grew up. Encouraged by the presence of a pastoral healthcare provider, she shared an earlier experience in which she had almost died and, in doing so, got in touch with her feelings. She came to a new insight about herself, and how God had been with her through it all. Although she knew that death was a possibility, she was aware that God was in charge of her situation. God was present in her previous crisis and would be with her now.

Jesus is our Emmanuel, our "God with us," until the end of time and throughout eternity. As spiritual caregivers learn to tap into the power of that presence through an authentic incarnational theology in their personal and professional life, they are able to provide an unencumbered, agendaless, non-anxious service to others by entering into their suffering and helping them to relate it to the Cross and Resurrection of Jesus.

Cross

Jesus says, "Blessed are you who weep now, for you will laugh" (Lk 6:21).[25] This is the paradox of the believer, that out of pain comes laughter. This can only be understood in the experience of the Kingdom. Even as Christians embrace the Cross and grieve their present situation,[26] they hope in the promise of Resurrection for the future. In Jesus' statement, "Blessed are those who mourn, for they will be comforted" (Mt 5:4),[27] we hear that grieving in the present prepares the way to joy in the future. Mourning accompanied by an anticipation of joy, is part of a theology of the Cross which culminates in the Resurrection.[28]

Jesus' life and sacrificial death is the model and salvific pattern for us all, reassuring us that our life and death freely given to God will be fully accepted and, on the last day, we, too, will rise triumphant from the grave. In Jesus' death on the Cross his message, his way of life, his very person were in fact rejected by the multitude and, to all appearances, he would seem to have failed in his life's project. Through the Resurrection, God not only endorsed his life and message but established the One rejected as the Universal Savior of humankind.[29]

On the Cross there is the 'death of God.' Here the human, finite, imperfect, weak and negative are assumed as divine elements in God's very self.[30] Human frailties are celebrated and proclaimed in the very person of God. When I learn to accept my frailties and humanness, I am able to see God's presence in myself and others. God's death validates all human weakness. So I do not have to be perfect nor deny my own brokenness and pain. However, many find it hard to deal honestly with their weaknesses, nor can they integrate their own pain — remaining aloof and distant. They tend to live through their professional role. Staying behind the mask of minister or teacher can get in the way of their being real with their clients. God's death on the Cross empowers us to be authentic with others. This Cross is a call, uniting the human experience of helplessness, humiliation or abandonment as intrinsically embraced — connected to the very heart of the Divine. Addressing itself to all people as the power of love — "made perfect in weakness" as St. Paul tells us (2 Cor 12:9)[31] — it is the Cross that touches suffering humanity.[32]

Whether a person is undergoing surgery, having medication for pain, living through loss with a loved one who has AIDS, having difficulty finding employment, going through a divorce, etc., everyone needs to be spoken to with love when they are suffering.

A number of years ago I knew a pastoral administrator who found it hard to deal with his faculty staff in difficult times. Whenever faculty members would share their vulnerabilities with him, he usually told a funny story and made light of the situation. When he received negative responses, he would just leave the conversation. Feeling uncomfortable with others' pain he was not willing or able to be with them in their emotional or spiritual distress. Because of his inability to confront his own anxiety and pain, he was not able to address the suffering of others, and any possibility of genuine relationship, healing or growth was lost.

Suffering

Suffering is a spiritual reality that forces us to review and re-evaluate our priorities and values[33] in life. Raising these values to consciousness helps us discern God's presence as a source of strength on our journey, assuring us that we are not alone. God in Jesus embraced human suffering, rejection, physical pain, emotional and spiritual anguish without reservation. The mystery of an incarnate and crucified God signifies for us that suffering is redemptive.

But for some who are unable to face the pain of their lives, overwhelmed by its sheer magnitude, suffering can be an obstacle to spiritual growth. In this framework, pastoral and spiritual care providers are challenged to show by their faith and presence the love and consolation of God in the midst of suffering. They are summoned and invited to engage their clients as unique and precious individuals in the sight of God who are in need of special care and healing. God's "suffering love" is there for every person yearning for salvation.[34]

God cares for and is united to all of us in our pain and difficulties. Spiritual care providers are challenged to administer a care that binds up wounds while uniting people. The Cross of Jesus bears what we cannot, all that is unspeakable in our lives. God is truly present with us in this suffering. Our belief in this great truth leads us to accept the gracious offer of the crucified

God to be with us always. As a community in God we respond by uniting ourselves with this loving God and with those who suffer.[35]

Recently, I ministered to the family and friends of a high school teacher who committed suicide on the school campus. The students and teachers went through a lot of pain and grief at his death. The hospital staff and chaplains spent time with the mourners allowing them to ventilate their anger, frustration, sadness and shock at his loss. Knowing they could not erase their pain, but only listen and console them, the staff brought the compassion of God to those who mourned. And God heard and accepted the pain, the complaints and the protests of those who were feeling abandoned. These grievers met the Divine who affirmed them in their anguish.

When people express their most intimate feelings and experiences, their relationship with the Divine becomes one of closest friend or trusted lover. God is more intimate in this relationship than the person is with himself/herself. As we see in the suffering of Job, and even more so in that of Jesus, God vindicates and validates the mystery of innocent suffering.[36] Whether a person speaks quietly or cries out in pain; whether he or she probes these mysteries or protests the injustice, whether one is defiant or subdued, resigned, outraged, melancholic or courageous, angry or accepting, friendly or distrustful, the Divine Listener hears the pain and weariness.[37] God is attentive to the individual and understands.

Suffering is unavoidably human, touching the deepest layers of the person. Suffering, while painful, is not always negative but can be a very important part of the growth toward wholeness.[38] Suffering points to the tension that exists in the human condition in which humans seek self-actualization on this earthly plane while awaiting the fullness of life eternal in God. It is the tension we all feel between this present existence and the life to come.[39]

When we enter fully into the human condition, we learn to

integrate suffering into our daily lives as we strive to cope with our co-dependencies, dysfunctional attitudes and behaviors. Having a realistic awareness of our own limits, we have the potential to enable others in their journey. In this sense, all spiritual care providers are "suffering healers." We heal as wounded healers[40] — with our own pains, shadows and sufferings. Recognizing that healing comes through a process of suffering, we persevere, sometimes surprised at our own inner capacity to suffer.[41] "Do not fear what you are about to suffer.... Be faithful until death, and I will give you the crown of life" (Rv 2:10).[42]

The pastoral and spiritual health provider who is open to others takes on their woundedness. Like the doctor who loses energy during surgery or the pastor who is tired after a marriage counseling session or the exhausted nurse repeatedly treating an infected wound, they have internalized some of the suffering of the person in their care.[43] Like Jesus who is the suffering servant, the caregiver is a part of God's healing process — a conduit of health.[44] In their creative ministry, the healer becomes another Christ. The goal is to have... "Christ be formed in you" (us)... (Gal 4:19) in order "to be conformed to the image of his Son" (Rm 8:29).[45]

A woman, driving behind him in another car, watched helplessly as her husband lost control of his car on an icy road. He spun out ramming into an embankment and two other vehicles. A truck skidded and slid sideways into the passenger side of her husband's vehicle, demolishing the passenger side of the car. She wondered about her husband's condition, fearful of the seriousness of his injuries. In time the scans and x-rays revealed that his leg was broken and needed surgery. He had a number of bruises and cuts but no life-threatening injuries. As I sat with her the woman spoke of another fear and anxiety. She was following her husband at a distance. Usually she would have been driving with him, sitting on the now wrecked passenger's side of the car. She would probably be critically injured or dead if she had been seated there. As I listened to her, mortality issues surfaced. She talked about her own near miss, the possibility of dying and leaving her three small children. She talked at length about her views and feelings associated with her own death.

Sensitivity to the pain of others catalyzes something real and human in us. We get in touch with the very soul of who we are and what we owe to Divine Providence. Spiritual healers are constantly aware that they live their lives in the presence of God who makes all things new.

Grieving

Limitations and finitude, beginnings and endings, are part of the created order. The Hubble telescope daily downloads powerful images to us on earth of gaseous clouds incubating and forming stars before our eyes. Within our galaxy stars are born, go through cataclysmic super-nova cycles and die. There is a continual cycle of birth and death that runs throughout creation. Grief and mourning are human responses to the finitude of all things. Loss and grief are integral to the way God has designed the universe. In creation we discover the Designer. We discover God in human grief.

With St. Augustine we realize that our hearts and souls are restless until they rest in God, the Alpha and Omega, the endpoint and culmination of all creation. God is "all" to everyone and everything (1 Cor 15:28). Thus, for the Christian, the loss of a loved one causes grieving, but it is not a grief without hope. Through the eyes of faith we can say with St. Paul that, in Christ, loss is transformed into gain (Ph 3:5-8). Even our own personal loss of life is a gain because of our anticipated eternal life with God.

St. Paul celebrates the imagery of both weakness and strength. It is in weakness that St. Paul believes that he is strong (2 Cor 12:10). Even though Paul is vulnerable in his body (2 Cor 12:10) and experiences hardship, disease and calamity (2 Cor

12:10), God's strength and power is present in the midst of weakness. In bearing the weakness and sorrow of others, pastoral and spiritual healthcare providers champion the be-attitudes of a Christian disciple who, in grieving, is grounded in God who is with us always.[46]

Resurrection

For the Christian, Jesus' Death and Resurrection is the basic pivotal and turning point of history, time and reality. All other experiences and realities in time and beyond time must be measured within this cosmic Divine mystery of life and death. In Jesus' Death, God is united to all human brokenness, failure, sadness, loss, physical suffering and death. It is the validation and final confirmation of God's presence in all human pain, tragedy, crisis, loss and grief. In Christ's Resurrection all human darkness and adversity are healed and raised to life — a new age has dawned.

The Resurrection is God's blessing on the world, a cosmic intervention to vindicate God's faithful and obedient servant (Lk 23:44)[47] — the Christ. From Christ flows the beginning of a new community with the new and continued mission of Jesus to all peoples (Lk 24:47).[48] The Christian community is called to care for all who are in pain (physical, mental, and spiritual), just as Jesus forgave the tax collector and the sinner (Lk 7:34), healed the centurion's servant (Lk 7:1-10), restored to life the only son of the widow of Naim (Lk 7:11-17), proclaimed liberty to captives... and set the downtrodden free (Lk 4:18).[49]

Led by Jesus, the Risen Lord, and sent forth by him (Mt 28:16-20), the Christian community reveals to those in need that "God is with us" (Emmanuel) (Mt 1:23)[50] and bears witness to this message with a certain awe and wonder (Mark 16:8).[51]

As caregivers we are guests in the lives of those who are served. We, like Jesus, become servant hosts (Lk 24:30) for our clients, patients, students and parishioners.[52] After His Resurrection Jesus commanded the disciples to carry out the Divine mission as witnesses (Acts 1:2, 8). In forgiveness and repentance the Christian community shares the resurrected power of Christ (Lk 24:47; 9:1; Acts 2:38; 3:12; 4:7; 6:8; and 19:11)[53] and facilitates a renewal of personal relations.[54] We are called to love one another as Jesus has loved us (Jn 15:12)[55] and to pray as He prayed to the Father on the night before He faced the agony of Golgotha:[56] "...that they may be one, as we are one, *I in them* and you in me, that they may become completely one" (Jn 17:23).[57] When the Christian community is "one," it fulfills Christ's will and is most effective in its service to others.

I recall an 80 year-old man who was admitted into the intensive care unit at the hospital following a heart attack. He pulled through, but was told by the doctor that without surgery he would soon have a repeat attack. He refused the surgery even though he knew that he would probably die within the next six months without it. He felt that at his age the trauma of open heart surgery and its recuperation would be "too much" to go through now. It just wasn't worth it to him. He was looking forward to "the fullness of life" which the Lord had promised to those were faithful to the end. After sharing his feelings with the nursing staff, he was supported in his decision.

The vocation of spiritual caregiving affirms life as an experience of Resurrection; therefore, choosing life is the care provider's deepest desire and motivation as he or she makes the stewardship of life an important part of their ministry and mission.[58] We share Jesus' vision of what is yet to be. This fullness of life is not yet, but coming to pass[59] — the reign of God is at hand and when it comes to pass we will all enjoy life in abundance.[60] Then we will see the incarnate resurrected Lord in the glory of His exaltation and enthronement.[61]

Hope

Through the Resurrection, all people will be transformed in Christ as all share in the fullness of God.

Once a woman with a brain aneurysm was brought by ambulance into the Emergency Department. Her husband of 45 years, grown children and grandchildren congregated in a waiting room to hear of her prognosis. When the physician came out, he informed the family that she had expired. They wept and expressed their sorrow at their loved one's death. Yet, there was a sense of hope in their grieving. Two of the sons asked me to pray for their deceased mother. A couple of the family members expressed their own prayers saying that they knew that their mother was alive and with God. The love and faith of this family was a clear sign of what Christ wants for His Church.

With an expectant faith, the Christian hope is that God "will wipe away every tear.... Death will be no more; mourning and crying and pain will be no more, for the first things have passed away" (Rv 21:4).[62] All pain will come to an end. Even suffering and death will not have the final say, but only God. As Christians have proclaimed over the millennia, "Our God Reigns!"

There was a family I counseled who had lost their little baby girl in a drowning. She had accidentally fallen into a family member's swimming pool. The horrible guilt and indescribable grief of her parents was profound. About four months later I met the parents at a church gathering. They were still grieving their child's death, but they knew that God was with them. They held fast to the hope that someday they would see their little girl again in the kingdom of God.

Jesus is the first fruit of the Resurrection. We who trust and hope in God will experience this eschatological event personally in the new Kingdom of God. All those who have loved, hoped, and had faith in the Divine shall be united to God. For all eternity they shall be transformed into partners of the very life of God.

Chapter Four

A SPIRITUALITY OF PRESENCE AND TRANSFORMATION

Jesus is the source of all pastoral presence, as well as the one who enters most fully into the lives of those experiencing loss. Pastoral care persons are called to be channels of his presence in their ministry with people. Their spirituality, therefore, is a spirituality of presence. A spirituality of presence moves beyond technique, beyond theory into praxis, into being with people at their worst — sharing their experience. By creating a safe place for them in their need, the pastoral caregiver helps to transform their grief into an opportunity for discerning God's voice in their unique experience of loss.

When we have not been willing to risk being with people in such situations, when we resist working with a person who is dying because of our own personal anxieties concerning death, we cannot be fully present to them. Healthcare professionals who do not enter into relationship with their clients, cannot offer a necessary sense of healing hospitality. We have to first learn to be comfortable with our own losses before we can be comfortable with what other's are suffering. Issues and losses that are not fully grieved, can emerge from our subconscious into consciousness. We may repress, deny, intellectualize, rationalize or sublimate these unhealed areas of concern and may act out these suppressed thoughts and feelings through avoidance and/or

hostile, defensive behaviors toward those receiving our care. Without examining our own motives, we may not be aware of our inner discomfort and how it affects the other person.

But when we respond to people by being genuinely present to them, our ability to serve grows in overall quality. Thus a spirituality of presence encompasses everything from the most rudimentary attending behavior to a sense of presence encompassed by the All in all. It is a spirituality that facilitate psycho-spiritual healing and growth in caregiver and client alike. Spiritual growth is as integral to all forms of caring and professional helping as conversion is for a mature relationship with God. Spiritual growth, healing and development are integral to our task of enabling persons to become all that God wants them to be. It presupposes a growing intimacy with the source of all transformation, Christ, who is the love of God incarnate. Those who are committed to this ministry are agents of His transforming power through their service to others.

Pastoral Presence in Grief/Bereavement Ministry

Mary of Bethany came out to where Jesus was and, seeing him, knelt at his feet and said, "Lord, if you had been here, my brother would not have died." When Jesus saw her weeping, and the Jews who came with her also weeping, he was greatly disturbed in spirit and profoundly moved (Jn 11:32-33)....[1] Jesus began to weep (Jn 11:35).[2] Not only did Jesus make himself the model of compassion for all those who mourn[3] but in his own Gethsemane, recognizing his own human need for the compassionate presence of others, he asked his friends to stay with him in the garden.

Pastoral care persons stay with the family who have lost a loved one, offering human presence and sharing their own vulnerability with those in need. We are with them in their shock, numbness, anger and whatever other emotions emerge to express their grief. As we remain with the bereaved, offering ourselves as strength and support in their pain, we share with them our quiet presence, vulnerability and feelings when appropriate. And we do so not by coercion or the use of the latest books or techniques, but by our genuine openness to their sensitivities, helping them discover who God is in their stories and their needs.[4]

A Spirituality of Presence

The pastoral care person evidences a spirituality of presence by being a companion, a friend who walks alongside, helping, sharing and sometimes just sitting empty-handed, watchful and available instead of running away — of just being there.[5] In being present to another, a depth of communication occurs, beyond words or style, technique, theory or theology. It is an awareness gifted by the Divine Presence.[6]

There is an integration of awareness which takes place for this Presence to materialize. It requires the caregiver to be conscious of both self and the other. With this awareness, we are free to focus fully on the person in front of us. To the degree that we are conscious of our own experiences, we are *more* available to be present to the consciousness of the other person.[7] In this way we embody a presence which enfleshes God's steadfast *love.* God is present in the dialogue between the grief or bereavement minister and those experiencing loss, pouring forth his grace and unconditional love,[8] remaining constant even when the other's personality becomes irritable and demanding, or when the person is dying — causing the caregiver's own grief to surface.

To remain present in such situations, the spiritual and emotional caregiver learns to balance intimacy and distance. Through 'being there' with an empathetic presence and developing professional objectivity, we promote an awareness of God's presence in the therapeutic relationship. In these graced moments, the spiritual caregiver becomes a flesh and blood symbol of the presence of God. Here, physical presence stimulates in the person primitive internal images that are part of an individual's intra-personal dynamics and internal resources. These images have strong unconscious forces connected to them that affect every aspect of a person's life[9] and how they relate in a therapeutic relationship between chaplain or minister and client.

A woman who was in the middle of a difficult divorce was being comforted by a spiritual friend. Gradually with this supportive friend as a source of strength, the woman was able to trust that God was with her in a supportive way. The companion was a catalyst who helped this individual to draw on her own internal beliefs and images of God as one who was supportive and trustworthy.

Spiritual, pastoral and emotional health care providers are central to therapeutic presence. We expand or diminish unconditional love with another, effectively or ineffectively, through holding on to, or letting go of, distortions and biases. We act as channels of love, offering our presence to those to whom we minister. Depending on whether or not we care for ourselves, we either benefit our clients — becoming effective sources of loving care — or we harm them. We become a focal point for God's constant love, or a vehicle of alienation. People will either resonate with, or be repelled by this encounter.

This ongoing unconditional love of God is offered to every person at every time and place. Through God's inner Word — gently speaking to us in the depths of our being — we reach for a God whose love is tangible in the person of Jesus Christ.[10] The basis of all pastoral presence is God's ever-present loving word. All pastoral care in grief and bereavement ministry relies on and manifests this Divine Presence.

Presence exists from the most basic attending behavior to that of intense mystical union. At the lowest level of presence, the caregiver mimics the other and may even do harm in his/

her mechanical style. But at the highest level of presence, there is a spiritual oneness and communion between the two people. They bond with one another and with the Transcendent in this deeply spiritual communication.[11] God wills that everyone abide in the Divine Presence,[12] therefore this Presence accompanies us in every possible human undertaking. God is with us in the eternal present moment.

A spirituality of presence constantly rediscovers the transcendence of God as the Presence within — an illumination shining forth from within the pastoral care person.[13] Our work is filtered through this presence, illuminating ourselves and others. Because religious experience has an individualized quality about it, pastoral care persons journey with others, respecting how spirituality grows out of each one's unique life experience. A spirituality of presence points to a willingness and a decision to assist persons in discovering God. Within their own understanding, their own interpretation of the events of their lives, the pastoring person helps people to recognize the presence of God within the context of their concrete life situation.[14]

This is the ideal; the reality is sometimes different. Recently at the hospital a Jehovah's Witness, in accord with her beliefs, chose not to receive a blood transfusion. The woman was in a car accident and was bleeding internally. Honoring the woman's request, the surgeon operated on her without giving her blood. When the woman came out of surgery, she was sent to the Critical Care Unit in a serious state. The physician there told her that she needed a blood transfusion. Her chances of recuperating would be very good if she received the blood — but without it she could die. The woman emphatically said no to receiving blood no matter the consequences. She felt at peace with herself as she chose to abide by her religious beliefs. The staff was sincerely afraid that she would die and became angry with her decision. They had difficulty respecting this patient's values. The chaplains listened to the frustration of the staff who were not willing to accept the person's religious choice and verbally shared their opposition. When an individual's choice does not fit the professional paradigm of care, when we don't agree with the morality of their choice, there is a temptation to push our choices and opinions rather insensitively onto others, rather then listening. In effect we devalue another when we devalue his/her beliefs and views about the situation. As long as a person's views are legal and will not harm another, we are called to honor the person, even if we choose not to participate in their care. We must respond to legal and moral limits while valuing the other's choice. But we must honor our own values as well. The balance is always a challenge needing great discernment and prayer.

Caregivers must learn not to stereotype their approach to the disease process — making it 'the normative approach' for all people. The context of caring must be individualized for each particular person. Learning to listen to stories, values, thoughts, meanings, desires, hopes and fears is integral to caring fully for people. Through being truly present to the other and by respecting their values, we provide spiritual and emotional care that empowers the other to approach the Divine. Through a spirituality of presence, people are encouraged to pursue their unique spiritual journey, guided to find their own meaning, understanding, interpretation and appreciation of the mystery of life and death. All the while they are encouraged to contemplate the mystery of God's Presence in their spiritual life.[15]

I remember a family whose father had died. The grown children had spoken to their father before his death, settling their issues — all but one daughter. I was aware of her anger and hostility as she said that she wanted to say some last words to her dead father. All the other family members left the room. When the primary nurse found out that she wanted to go into the room with the dead man alone, she forbade it. It was against hospital policy and protocol. I intervened, explaining how important it was for her to have closure with her father to grieve the death. She relented. We trusted her to know her own needs better than we did, and gave her the opportunity to get in touch with those issues that were important to her. The result was a visible peace of mind and spirit. Obviously there was a need for this young woman to vent her feelings towards her father. She would still need more time for further resolution of her issues, and she was encouraged to have some follow-up counseling. But at that moment, it was important that she begin to resolve some of her anger.

To offer genuine care, we need to be aware of our own, and our client's, mind and spirit. When we are in touch with ourselves, the client's desires and best interests can be served. A spirituality of presence promotes everyone as a special earthen vessel of God, with a personal and unique journey into mystery. While advancing another's passage, each pastoral care provider must be cognizant of the challenge this can be to their own personal spiritual development and growth.

Facilitating Psycho-spiritual Healing and Growth

Traditionally the pastoral care provider's working premise is that spiritual growth is an essential objective in all caring and counseling; that a growth relationship with God is an indispensable aspect of total wholeness.[16] Pastoral care enables spiritual wholeness throughout the various transitions and passages of the life cycle. Building on life cycles and focusing attention on the stages of faith development in the spiritual formation process,[17] we strive to assist people in the appropriation of faith within the context of their life situations.[18]

I remember visiting an elderly man who was prepared to die. His wife had died three years earlier. "I am ready to meet my God and know my Savior," he told me. He had been suffering from kidney failure for the last five years, receiving renal dialysis three times a week. Two previous attempts at kidney transplants had failed, and he was getting progressively weaker and worse. He had taken care of all the provisions of his estate, leaving everything to his daughter and did not want to continue his dialysis treatment, saying he had suffered enough. His physician and the nursing personnel would not hear his plea. Hoping for a successful kidney transplant, they were trying to get him to continue his treatment.

After listening and praying with him and with his daughter, I relayed to the staff his intentions to continue with comfort medications, fluid and nutrition, but that he wanted no more dialysis. He could not endure the burden and suffering any longer. The staff heard his wishes and relinquished their aggressive medical treatment, honoring and respecting his decision. Within four days after this ethical decision-making process, he died peacefully with his intentions, needs and values respected.

This approach of respecting other's wants and desires brings about spiritual healing. Such spiritual and emotional caregivers promote a connection between the mind and the body through the integration of the spirit and are instruments of growth and psycho-spiritual healing. To be effective, though, we need to be in an ongoing state of conversion ourselves, transformed by God into hopeful, loving persons who offer their service to others.[19] The caregiver should be a person who is actively engaged in personal healing and conversion, who sees life through the mind and heart of God. He or she must be aware of human limitations and the knowledge gleaned from current scientific studies, while having a greater sense of one's dependence on God's loving presence.[20] This conversion process involves a deepening self-appropriation, self-knowledge, self-discovery and self-understanding.[21] In recognizing our need for conversion we are reminded of our own brokenness, mortality and our need for healing. This vulnerability can help us to become non-judgmental channels for growth and healing for self and others. Our personal woundedness becomes an effective instrument of Christ's life-giving healing.[22]

When we react hastily to anyone who 'pushes our buttons,' when we feel overpowered and overwhelmed, and easily triggered by the others' 'woundedness,' we are not effective. When we are able to love and help those who are angry, complaining or negative, then we ourselves are in the process of conversion and not dominated by their brokenness. Those who over-identify their issues with those they treat allow their own vulnerabilities and sensitivities to get in the way of good caregiving. We must allow ourselves to be more accepting of our imperfections, to foster a healthy detachment from the others' issues and experiences in order to have enough objectivity to serve.

Those who assert themselves aggressively, who challenge every statement made to them, are harboring a deep seated insecurity. Defensiveness, anxiety, stiffness, guardedness, tension and utter seriousness, inhibit us as effective caregivers. We do not need to be perfect, but we do need to be persons who are actively learning how to channel our shadow side in healthy ways. Understanding ourselves as human beings created in the image and likeness of God — possessing the dignity of those for whom Christ lived, died and rose unto everlasting life — empowers us to love ourselves. For this reason the spiritual/pastoral and emotional caregiver ought to be one who is forgiving of personal deficiencies and failures, accepting the gift of Divine forgiveness that God has bestowed upon us in Christ.[23]

It is those who are willing to be forgiven who can forgive others. When working with people who are difficult, abrasive, and complaining, we are challenged to value the virtue of acceptance and forgiveness. Through forgiving oneself and others, an attitude and way of being surfaces which allows people to be human. Life is seen in its correct perspective, one in which people are understood as creatures in relationship with one another, and a forgiving Creator.

Cultivation of an attitude of prayer energizes the work and tasks of one's caregiving, and acts as a springboard for psycho-spiritual healing. This healing presence permeates us as we perform our duties and offer our ministry of service. In recognizing the value of prayer and explicitly prayer for those with whom we work, we recall how Jesus — who kept an extremely active life — prayed in the synagogues, or spent whole nights in solitary prayer.[24] We rely on God as the source of our strength, the ultimate source of our self-development and of our work with others. In prayer, we recognize our reliance on God, acknowledging that God is in charge, and that all is gift.[25]

A Spirituality Of Transformation

Coming to terms with one's giftedness and ongoing conversion is necessary for Christian spiritual transformation. The goal of transformation is to form Christ in one's personality, in every aspect of oneself, and in the community of bonded persons. The result of this conversion process, is new life which leaves the impression of the transforming love of God on everything and everyone it touches.[26] As ministers of transformation, we are carriers of hope and comfort to those who find themselves in a place of mourning (Mt 5:3). Like Jesus, those who offer this service are ministers of messianic restoration (Is 61:1, 2-3).

One night I was paged to come to the hospital for a man who was dying from a brain tumor. He and his wife were having a big family reunion with all his six grown children at home who had traveled long distances to attend. One of the sons came in from Alaska, while another daughter came from Nuremberg, where for the past few years she had been teaching English. The man and his wife had been married for 45 years. That night at the end of the festivities, he went to the bathroom and didn't come out. His wife went to check on him and found him slumped over on the floor. She called Emergency 911, and soon he was in the hospital. A neurosurgeon said that the brain scan revealed an inoperable, fatal brain tumor.

When I arrived at the hospital, all of the adult children and their spouses were there with their mother. Teary eyed and sobbing, some of them were reading the Bible while others were praying the rosary. At the family's request, I contacted a priest, who prayed for the man for forgiveness of any possible sins (sacramental conditional absolution) and prayed for healing and preparation for death (sacramental anointing of the sick). After the priest left, I stayed with the family to continue ministering to their needs, as they silently prayed for their father at his bed in the Neuro-Intensive Care Unit. He remained unconscious and within a short time his vital signs worsened. Within the hour he died with his family at his side.

When it was appropriate, I offered a prayer for all of them. As I listened to the family members, I sensed sadness, yet trust in God, in the midst of their pain — a strength that came from within each person. Darkness was dispelled by an inner light, as their faith in God, their love for their father, and one another, guided their path.

The transcendent light of Christ reaches into each person, breaking into their lives through the actions of Jesus. The healings, exorcisms and miracles of Jesus are evidence of God's reign breaking into and touching human lives and every dimension of the world, restoring creation to its original purpose.[27] To remain faithful to Jesus' restoration, the community envelops all those who are broken within an atmosphere of healing, restoring people and relationships, and offering hope to those in need.

Those who are unwilling to be transformative agents often 'get stuck,' become depressed, blame, and deny their responsibility as agents of change. Seeing themselves as victims, they almost invariably become disillusioned in the helping environment, and eventually face some level of failure in their caregiving to others. That is why it is so important that in developing new methods of personal healing and growth for themselves and their clients, they try to strike a balance between issues of wholeness and holiness.

The pastoral care person strives to become conscious of the dynamic relationship between spiritual growth and transformation in God, and personal maturity. Through this ongoing process, one's life evidences integration, interior freedom, deepened faith commitment and intense but balanced apostolic involvement. There is a need to respect one's autonomy, self-actualization and self-transcendence as a precious gift of God[28] providing the individual with genuine human freedom and empowering him or her to make and live mature choices. We are challenged to recognize the uniqueness of everyone's spirituality and story, striving to affirm what is best for each person — letting go of anything that does not respect their humanity.[29]

Caregivers who feel strongly about their convictions being right, cannot force them on others assuming that their personal, cultural or religious values should be imposed as normative for all.[30] In order to offer the best possible care, we must be willing to accompany all our clients, Christian, Jewish, Buddhist, Native and Tribal Religious, Islamic or whatever, as they work through their grief in ways they best understand.

If one is uncomfortable with loud demonstrative crying, or even wailing, which is a part of the cultural expression of some ethnic groups, he/she will find it difficult to value the different ways that individuals from various cultures or religious groups mourn. But spiritual caregivers who learn to accept and transcend their own culture develop a healthy spirituality and become truly effective healers.[31] By becoming skilled in the classical spiritual disciplines and the ancient tradition of spiritual guidance, pastoral care persons and pastoral counselors practice a ministry that enhances spiritual awareness at every age and stage and in every circumstance of life.[32]

A spirituality of transformation aims to lead a person into a permanent state of God-consciousness — a permanent state of transpersonal consciousness or being alert to the union between your true self and the One in whom all things are held together (Col 1:17).[33] It draws a person into a connection with the transcendent Source within their religious heritage. People who reach this vantage point notice that they are being changed.

One woman who wanted to be certified in the art of pastoral care at her parish changed from always blaming others for her mistakes — being very judgmental and angry about life — to greater acceptance and inner peace. Over a three year period of her receiving spiritual direction and counseling, she let go of the burdensome irrational attitudes which weighed her down. She realized that it was she who had created an unhappy and frustrated person. In realizing that she could be more accepting of others and herself, she began to see herself in a new light. She spent some time each day in prayer and found healthy outlets. She discovered God in others and within herself, changing because of her commitment to do so. It was really gratifying to watch her grow in her journey as caregiver.

Acting as channels of a spiritual regeneration based on the life, death, and transformation of Jesus Christ through his Resurrection, we draw upon our physical, psycho-social, and spiritual resources to attend to others in need. Recognizing that all transformation at its source is a divine gift, caregivers try to help others transform their desires and decisions, bringing them into union and harmony with the will of God.[34]

Because God has shed divine blood for all, people can change. They can be transformed individually, communally and cosmically into the body of Christ.[35] Because the Spirit blows where He wills, all people have access to this transformative spirituality: Christians as members of the Body of Christ, followers of Islam as the Faithful, Jews as the People, Buddhists as the Sangha.[36]

According to Douglas John Hall, through partaking in the divine plan of renewal, the pastoral care person is a witness to God's mending of life itself, to the very mending of creation.[37] Focusing one's energies, by becoming a mediator of the spiritual re-creation and regeneration of human beings, spiritual guides — Abbas and Ammas — act as special instruments in the direction of others to God. Participating in the re-creative work of God, they awaken and quicken in others the life of the Spirit.[38]

Responding as brothers, sisters, fathers, mothers, friends,

companions, guides, midwives, teachers and counselors to those whose lives we have connected with, each spiritual care provider co-journeys with the other. We attempt to respect the other's life direction, assisting them to become *mystics* within their own spiritual and/or religious traditions, while intentionally attending to our own spiritual progress. This is accomplished by the spiritualization of ordinary life — the daily awareness of the presence of God in all we do.[39]

While covenanted to foster full humanity, and self-intimacy, we are called to help people experience the mystery of who they really are. While fostering self-intimacy, we attune people to the diverse facets of their being through promoting their physical, mental, emotional, spiritual health and well-being.[40] We become resources for others to help them discover their higher Self. By centering our growth on our own higher Self, we too experience the transformation of our existential person.[41]

To reach our goal of empowering caregivers to become resources of transformation and healing, continuing pastoral education programs and other pastoral resources must be developed to teach caregivers to lead people to discover that God is within. Our hospitals, churches and schools must become environments of love, understanding and skill where pastoral care providers are empowered to be the kind of ministers God has called them to be.

This was made tangible for me some time ago after my wife and I were rear-ended by a drunk driver hitting us at about 50 miles per hour. We were thrown about 150 feet across the oncoming traffic into a snow bank. Our car was totaled, and we were in shock. When we arrived at the Emergency Room at St. Charles Medical Center, the nursing staff and physician on duty were very caring towards us. Each member of the staff was really attentive, responding to our needs and hearing our emotional pain. Even though we were disoriented from our traumatic accident, we found the staff to be extraordinarily responsive to us in our conscious spoken and unconscious unspoken needs.

Besides taking x-rays and checking us for internal injuries and concussions, they gave us space to express our feelings and concerns as we chose, providing us with an opportunity to reflect calmly on the events that had transpired. Our car was a tangled mess, and we were both hurt; but God was with us through the whole incident from beginning to end, not least of all in the persons who were our caregivers.

Chapter Five

IMPLICATIONS FOR CAREGIVERS IN THE MINISTRY OF GRIEF

My personal grief ministry began when I was 16 years of age. It was at my grandmother's funeral where I sat next to my mother who sobbed and wept bitterly at the loss of her best friend. The casket was in the front of the church and I was sitting in the first row pew with my family. Grieving friends and extended family members streamed by the casket in a solemn line to say their good-byes. The mourners walked in cautious unison — as if choreographed by an unknown director, as they offered us a word of comfort. The solemn procession stopped before each person in my family as I watched from my station in that grief-stricken row of mourners. They hugged us and offered condolences as the slow moving train of grief methodically passed by us.

Well-meaning persons mumbled customary platitudes of comfort to my mother and the family. Floating in a kind of a fog which permeated our ability to think, listen or respond, we didn't really see or hear them: "She is out of this valley of problems." "She was a good woman; she struggled hard, and now she is at peace." "Don't worry you'll see her again." "She's in a better place." "Thank God, she's out of her suffering and pain." "It will be O.K."

They wanted to say something to us, to alleviate the pain, theirs and ours. And as a result they felt better for going through the funeral ritual. They were kind and loving people doing what they presumed would be helpful. Yet, after their words trailed off into the gloomy atmosphere of the room, the abiding pain remained.

At the cemetery the tone once again was solemn, and we all cried. Leaving the gravesite, we went to my grandmother's home where a lot of food had been prepared as a special way to honor her memory. She was known for her many large festive holiday dinners.

Later my mother, aunts and uncles told stories and expressed their deepest feelings about grandmother. As they shared their stories and emotionally charged experiences with one another, they expressed their sorrow at her loss in their own unique way.

In reflecting upon all this, I have come to appreciate the value of creating safe and comfortable places where people are free to talk about what's happening to them. Grievers heal when they encounter listeners who value being totally present to the other: their mind, their emotions and their whole being, body and soul.

Implications for the Pastoral Listener

Attending is a necessary ingredient for listening — hearing what is behind the forced smile or the pleasant conversation. Attending includes verbal and non-verbal skills of eye contact, body language (movement and gestures), physical space, and the manifestation of an awareness of feelings being expressed in silent gestures. It is not just the facts, but the way persons convey them, that point to their needs, issues, and meanings. People who truly listen, read the body language and speech as symptoms of the soul, of what is deep within. If caregivers are preoccupied with their own needs, then they miss this opportunity to offer healing. Through helping people clarify their experiences, feelings, thoughts and resulting actions, caregivers are agents of freedom who help people celebrate their stories.

When caregivers journey with people into the deeper levels of feelings, they become catalysts of change and transformation bringing relief and new awareness through their listening presence. Consider the woman who is waiting to hear a diagnosis for a critical condition. The response from the doctor does not come as quickly as she would like. She becomes angry and targets the parish minister with her frustration. By listening to her feelings, the minister acts as a safety valve. Her anger changes to sadness, and finally the true emotion of fear about the possibility of dying surfaces. Mortality is the real issue.

When caregivers are at ease with their own feelings, they provide comfort to others. Learning to accept cultural, familial, religious/spiritual and social differences in people's affective expression, opens the caregiver to the privilege of observing a kaleidoscope of emotions in an individual's unique story and situation. But the opposite is also true. When the caregiver has difficulty being with others from different cultural and value frameworks, he/she manifests judgments and stereotypes in the performance of their tasks.[1]

Mind-Body Connections and Emotions

Through affective hearing — linking a person's emotions to overall health — the caregiver delivers effective (w)holistic care. Bill Moyers hosted a program dealing with "The Mind-Body Connection" in which researchers discussed the correlation of the emotions with one's physical health.[2]

Dr. Candace Pert explained this connection:

> Feelings and thoughts bring activity in the brain and with it a cascade of physical changes in the body. The biochemicals of emotions are neuro-peptides. They are found in the part of the brain that mediates emotion, and

> are released during certain emotional states. Emotions seem to be the currency in which the mind and matter inter-convert. Emotions are stored in the body in the peptides, receptors, cells, and called up by the mind.[3]

Scientists have located nerves in the immune system. This leads to the conclusion that the nervous system might be controlling some immune response. Consequently, the immune system and the nervous system are not independent but possibly affect one another.[4] Studies in biofeedback using the Galvanic Skin Response point to a connection between the mind and the body.[5]

From my pastoral observations people experience healing when we practice effective emotional listening. When we deal with people as persons — not test tube experiments or objects — pastoral listeners are like good medicine. When we approach those in our care with the dignity of personhood, we stimulate and enliven a process of healing that releases to a fuller degree the physical, emotional, spiritual, mental and social potential of each individual.

An Empathetic Manner of Care

Developing a manner of empathetic care, we attend to the whole person — their thoughts, feelings, actions, choices and relationships. Our call and skills summon us to move beyond our professional role and therapeutic insights into 'real presence.' When we choose to set aside a purely clinical agenda, refraining from making judgments for the moment, walking in the shoes of the client, responding in a flexible and tentative manner, the person has the opportunity to safely explore their ideas and feelings. The central ingredient of the counseling process (communication and listening) is the counselor's (listener's) ability to perceive and communicate accurately and with sensitivity the feelings of the person and the meaning of those feelings.[6] We know that we are truly attuned to them when their response to us is, "Yes, that's what I said," or "Yes, that's what I meant."

In the film *Beaches*[7] Hilary Whitney (Barbara Hershey) becomes sick, passes out, and is rushed to the hospital. Her friend, C.C. Bloom (Bette Midler) cancels her concert performance and immediately drives from Los Angeles to San Francisco. When C.C. arrives, Hilary is dying in the intensive care unit. She pleads to spend her last hours on earth at her beach house. C.C. readily takes her there.

The two friends sit together on the veranda. Hilary watches her daughter play on the sand of the beach as the ocean waves flow in and out. C.C. touches Hilary tenderly on her arm and looks over at her, truly listening to her friend, even though she isn't saying anything. A tear wells up in C.C.'s eye. Hilary turns her head toward C.C.'s loving smiling face, and in the silence of the moment more is spoken than in their many verbal conversations shared throughout the years of their friendship. In that moment C.C. was truly there for her, offering genuine spiritual support.

Grief and Pastoral Counseling

Although, much of the paradigm for therapeutic persons and clinical practice is to treat pathology and symptoms of disease and not the whole person,[8] spiritual care providers can enable people to attain wholeness. The caregiver can foster positive personal relationships, heal institutional relationships, facilitate the expression of emotions and the completion of unfinished business associated with the loss of a loved one.

To finish their grief work, people must fully embrace the reality of the loss, deal with both verbalized and dormant affect, surmount various hindrances to future readjustment and create a healthy emotional retreat from the loss. Finally as healing progresses those in grief begin to feel more comfortable as they begin to reinvest their emotions in other things and relationships.[9] These tasks are best worked on within the framework of the faith perspective and beliefs/values of a person's life.

All people are in need of non-judgmental and supportive care after a loss. Those who lose a loved one and have no social support network especially need assistance, as do those who find themselves in a concurrent life crisis.[10] Those who are committed to and skilled in facilitating spiritual care, can help the grieving through this process.

Helper's Guidelines for the Resolution of Grief

Grief at times can make people feel that they are flipping out or going crazy. By reaching out and giving people permission and time to grieve, caregivers help to validate the normalcy of the grief experience. We provide people with the space to grieve in their own way respecting different expressions. This can be extremely liberating for family and friends. Human beings do not have to grieve all in the same way like clones. In assessing people's defense mechanisms and coping styles to determine the level of their effectiveness, the care provider notices if the grieving person has a tendency to let go, or to hold on to the loss. Are his or her ways of dealing with the loss healthy or unhealthy? Developing bonds with people opens the door for facilitating the grief process.

If our assessments suggest pathology, the rest of the team should be informed, and a psychiatric evaluation may be appropriate. Other means might likewise be suggested, e.g., support groups (Compassionate Friends, Grief Recovery Seminars), counselors, pastoral grief counselors and therapists to continue healing, the sharing of resources, etc.

A Pastoral Grief Intervention

One night a three-year-old was brought to the Emergency Department by the paramedics. She had been playing outside at her parents home, wandered off into a pond, and was found floating on the water by her mother. The mother had administered CPR for about fifteen minutes until the ambulance arrived on the scene.

When I got to the hospital the baby was lying on a gurney in the trauma room. The father and mother were standing there crying in deep pain as they stared at their dead baby. I introduced myself as the Chaplain. The father stood there motionless and looked at me with his tear stained eyes like a knife was going through his very soul. The mother was sobbing softly, holding her baby. She said, "I don't want you to go. This is not really happening." I validated the mother's emotional state saying, "This is painfully unreal." Then the mother said, "I'm going to wake up. Please let me wake up. This is not happening." Again I offered her validation by responding, "This is an awful nightmare." Then she put her arms around her baby girl and hugged her.

I touched the baby's father with my right hand in a gesture of comfort. He looked at me with a blank stare, not saying anything. I let them know I would stay with them. The baby's mother said, "She is a part of me, and she is gone. Now what am I going to do without her? She was so special to me." While looking directly at her baby, she said, "You depended on me, and I let you down." I responded, "You feel guilty that you were not able to help her." She said, "Yes, I do; I couldn't revive her." I allowed her to express her feelings further by responding, "You blame yourself for not saving her life." She responded affirmatively, and we spoke about her sense of guilt for the next few minutes. Without discounting her feelings I assured her that she had done all that she could. It wasn't her fault. During our dialogue I placed my hand on her shoulder allowing myself to sigh as I entered into their grief at this painful loss. She sensed I was with her in her pain and gave me a nod of approval. Then she began to quiet down.

I went over to the baby's father who had been silent through most of the time and asked how he was doing. He began to talk about his feelings of helplessness, not knowing what to say to comfort his wife. For the next ten minutes, we talked about his feelings until he seemed to experience some relief, and took my hand holding it tightly.

I spent another hour with this couple. After awhile other relatives came to lend support, and one of the grandmothers asked me to say a prayer. Gathering the parents and the family members together I said a prayer for the little girl who was now with Jesus, thanked God for her brief but special life which had touched us all, and prayed for Jesus to be with each person in their pain and grief.

I offered the parents a bereavement folder. It was developed by the Pastoral Care Department to address issues around the loss a loved one, such as how to survive your loss, responses to grief, the stages of grief, ideas for journal writing, suggestions for coping with holidays, some commonly shared feelings, the loss of a child, resources in the community, etc.[11] I told them about Compassionate Friends, a support group for parents who have lost a child. I gave them my card if they wanted to talk at a later time. The child's father shook my hand and thanked me. The mother hugged and thanked me, as did other family members. One said, "Your presence has been helpful." I said goodbye encouraging them to be supportive to one another, assuring them of my prayers. Walking out through the hospital lobby I passed a wall mural with the following statement: "Our doors will remain open always. We are here with our presence in your midst to serve you and through you, our God."[12] Experiences like these are most difficult to live through for everyone involved, including the caregiver.[13]

Caring for the Caregiver

Caregivers need to find ways of dealing with such traumatic experiences. I have developed several techniques for such times. The first step is always to give these situations of trauma and pain to God in prayer. I try to express what I'm truly feeling and thinking, letting go of the situation and placing all those involved in the loving hands of God. In doing this I become aware of how much God loves these persons who are hurting, and at the same time I realize how much God is caring for my needs too.

While I am in the actual situation of trauma, I try to be always fully present, using all my pastoral skills as I call upon divine assistance. I am with them in the moment, and am concerned with helping them through my compassion and my presence. At the same time, I have come to realize that no matter what happens ultimately this traumatic situation is really in God's care. As I sit in prayer I give it all over to God, aware that God is God. God is the savior, and I am not! I experience myself as a creature — a child of God — loved by the Creator, and so I feel free to let go of holding on to those whom I have helped.

I find support when I talk about my personal needs with a minister who serves as a supervisor for me. We meet regularly to discuss my feelings, thoughts and problems related to pastoral situations. I participate in a clergy and ministers pastoral support group as a vehicle of my self-care. I exercise, relax and pray regularly. The key to healthy self-care is the realization that I am one person with my own spiritual, emotional and physical gifts and limits. I must set healthy boundaries on my energies. I have limited resources.

We need to take time for ourselves, even at times saying to people, "I am not able to help you now." Many caregivers believe it is their responsibility to take care of others, no matter what. They feel that if they don't do it, it won't be done. They place unhealthy expectations and excessive burdens on themselves as caregivers. They choose to stay in caregiver roles even outside their pastoral work. They bring the caregiving role home — finding it difficult to separate themselves from their own expectations. Sometimes the caregiving role started in their families of origin. In their family they were caregivers, and they still hold on to this self-image as the core element of their identities.

We sometimes forget our human limits and boundaries finding ourselves in the helper role and having a majority of relationships in which we function primarily as helper. We need to change this and develop relationships of equality, mutuality and nurturance. It is of paramount importance that we develop attitudes and ways of caring for ourselves. Without such, we can expect to find ourselves edgy, sick, ineffective, tired or exhausted from our pastoral interventions. We may even find ourselves in a personal crisis that challenges our very choice of vocation. The following is a poem addressing the minister's need to discern God's call.

Call of the Spirit:
Reflections on Pastoral Ministry

Tugging,
Insistent.
The Spirit gently pulls on that part of me that yearns to be left alone.
Embracing the vision of unknown horizons
not yet created,
she dares to offer visions of the possible tomorrow.
Childlike expectations dance across the memory
like the hypnotic pattern of flashing lights on a Christmas tree:
Off, on.
There it is.
Now its gone.
Teasing.

Tempting.
She subtly lures the heart with joy once tasted —
Hope for tomorrow.
"You can help. You have the gift. You can heal their pain."
Worn out.
Weary by knowing what her call demands,
I try to close my ears to her song,
Oh yes, I've been on this road before.
I'll ignore her irritating tempting with self indulgence.
Maybe she'll go away.
Remembering the wear and tear,
the exhausted days and nights ahead if I acknowledge her request,
I avert her gaze.
Languishing in sweet denial,
Pretending that the call of her eternal heartbeat is but the ticking of the hall clock,
I drown the constant itch of her breath with chocolate,
the seduction of her voice in the diversion of yet another cup of coffee.
Surely I should wash the floor,
Call my mother,
Write to my daughter ,
Take a walk with my husband. . . .
But there she is again,
in the clean surface of the linoleum,
in the warmth of my mother's voice,
in the very thought of my girl,
in the soft eyes of my husband,
she dances to the tune of renewed hope for the day.
Her music surges.
Seeps into,
Penetrates my soul,
Unravels the well-worked weave of denial

and invades into the very pores of my spirit.
Alas!
There is no escape!
All resistance is laid waste.
Her love has managed to move into the essence of who I am
singing her ever-present song of possibility.
"If only someone would care for my broken ones, it could be different. The world will change
You have the gift. Will you be my voice, my hands, my healing touch?"
Hearing the hypnotic Eros of her song I rise to try again.
Knowing that she will do the work, if I just be her channel (O'Connell-Roussell, '96).[13]

Caregivers who are committed to (w)holistic self-care choose to deal with their issues of co-dependency,[14] to let go of irrational thinking patterns with their ensuing behaviors,[15] and to build healthy collaborative relationships where mutual assertiveness is valued.[16] Adopting self-care attitudes and behaviors, engaging in methods of relaxation, self-hypnosis, meditation, autogenic exercises (teaching the body and mind to respond to verbal commands and relax), imagination, coping skills training, biofeedback, breathing, time management and thought stopping[17] are all part of keeping the caregiver centered and whole.

As we've previously discussed, many professionals are taught to treat people's symptoms through the use of external agents or interventions — drugs, etc. This is the approach of much of the Western model of treatment/care which is at odds with (w)holistic healing,[18] including self-care. Because of this tendency in our society, it is critical that caregivers move toward balance in their approach to self-care. In accepting the (w)holistic challenge, we will model healing for those for whom we wish to be agents of care.

Can I tolerate my own personal tensions, experiencing both

moments of dying and living? If not how can I care for people in their tensions as they struggle between resistance and acceptance? Am I convinced, as was St. Paul, "that neither death, nor life... nor things present, nor things to come... will be able to separate us from the love of God in Christ Jesus, our Lord" (Rm 8:38-39)?[19]

As a young man, I struggled with the image and the need to look like I had it all together. I thought I was one of the few in my circle with this problem. I put emphasis on my strengths while I kept my weaknesses hidden away in the shadows.

One night I dreamed of a large oval table that filled a dining room. People came in and sat around the table: a Native American shaman, a young man blonde and strong, a long black-haired woman, a sinister-looking brown-skinned Mexican, an Asian with black wavy hair and dark beard, a large Snoopy dog, a man who kept talking in a friendly manner, another who read a book at the table, a man who was in a quiet and reflective mood and myself as I appeared in life (a young man in my mid-twenties). We were waiting for one more character to join us at the table.

A black-haired man with a cane came in limping. I was quite surprised to see him there and wondered how he had managed to get into the room. He sat down at the table with the others.

After awaking, I felt that this dream was telling me something about myself. Each of the personages represented aspects of my life. I was a healer, a strong independent individual, a man who related to the feminine within, a person of mixed ethnicity, a playful jokester on occasion, a friendly conversationalist, a student, a praying person and, finally, my composite perception of myself. I was also the person with weaknesses who had limped into the room. The dining room and table represented the fact that each of the personages in my dream needed to be nourished to become whole. It was important that I accept these images of myself and not suppress them. Such symbols and stories emerge out of the depths of our souls and reveal how we look at ourselves as sons and daughters of God.

I recall a man at death's door who had lost the will to live. Gradually, he discovered the courage to look inside himself, and what he saw was a vast and empty void. It was scary to contemplate. At first it seemed like a bottomless pit to him. Eventually, out of the murky black hole, he saw the figure of a small, happy child emerge. This image gave him a series of insights about his problems and his life. Over time he came to understand that God saw him as a unique and valuable work of His hand. He was a child of God worthy of life and love. He realized in the midst of his darkness that God was with him. A change began to take place in him over a period of months as he slowly recovered his health and zest for life. He knew that God was alive and active in the core of his soul. He had found the buried treasure of God's life within himself (cf. Mt 13:44).

Obviously, there are stories in which people do not get better. There is no magic wand or technique that works for everyone and it is God alone who, ultimately, holds all the answers.

Conclusion

As agents of spiritual and emotional transformation, we are not alone. The findings from quantum physics speak to the relationship between the observer and the participant in the universe and how we profoundly affect one another. Today, as we reflect on the practice of pastoral care, we look to the universe for our example. Light from a distant star reaches us on the earth. After having traveled aeons, billions of light years, witnessing the genesis of stellar and planetary bodies, this light joins us. Let us journey with this traveler from the very beginning of time.

After the big bang, clouds of gases and energy are released. These clouds and primal elements give birth to the first stars.

Older supernovas furnish the building blocks of later successor and progeny stars. These stars cluster together into galaxies. A star in a portion of the Milky Way galaxy becomes a supernova, the precursor to the sun. Planets and moons take shape. Our planet, Earth, develops oceans, atmosphere and land masses. Life begins to form in the sea. Gradually more complex creatures appear, mammals evolve and the first humans emerge on the scene. Over aeons of time you and I arrive in the 20th century. We have a connection to our great-grandparents, the stars. We are star stuff. The stars are part of us.

We are in relationship with all that is, and all that is in us. We are agents of spiritual transformation who are, at one and the same time, participants and observers, prisms of the divine, co-creators with God and others in an adventure where all is continually being made new. We are involved in the ongoing process of these dynamic inner relationships, calling us to become the beings of love and light that God, from all eternity, has wanted us to be.

As we integrate into our lives the healing vision offered here, and act as effective channels of God's presence, we begin to give shape to how pastoral care will be practiced in the future. Spiritual caregivers are choosing a process of spiritual and emotional empowerment, healing and transformation for themselves and others journeying through loss, grief and bereavement. This community is discovering its heart, its spirit, its past, present and future by celebrating and embodying God's Presence — His Life, Death and Resurrection — whenever and wherever it serves. Its members look forward with St. Paul to the time when all things are subjected to Christ. "Then the Son Himself will also be subjected to the One who put all things in subjection under Him, so that God may be all in all" (1 Cor 15:28).[20]

Appendix A

PASTORAL RESOURCES FOR GRIEF MINISTERS

The purpose of these pastoral resources is to help caregivers deal with grief effectively in performing their ministries and in their daily living.[1] This material addresses values, belief systems and cultural milieu (including behavioral and social sciences, medical information, pastoral resources) as well as human experiences.[2] The following questions below will help caregivers evaluate their efforts.

A Self-Evaluation of the Communication of Empathy

Think about a recent situation when you acted as a caregiver, listening to someone share anger, sadness, loneliness, happiness, etc., with you. Reflect on the following questions about how you were present and actually listened to those to whom you offered care. Share your insights in your journal, in pairs, small groups or in a large group discussion.

1. Did you suitably reply to what the person was saying? What was especially pertinent about the encounter that took place? List ways in which the person revealed that you appropriately heard what they were trying to communicate regarding their experience, such as verbally, through nods, etc.

2. What did you pick up from their body language?
3. In what ways did you hear and comprehend the person's feelings? In what ways did you incorrectly evaluate their feelings or situation?
4. Did you authentically hear and discern the magnitude of the person's feelings? Did you pick up the degree of their anger, sadness, fear, etc.? Did you fully perceive the depth of their sense of loss?
5. When talking about losses previously faced, how did the individual say they differed from or were similar to what he or she was feeling on this occasion?
6. What is at the heart of what this person was expressing?
7. Is what I say in such situations my own point of view or do I do my utmost to impart to this person what I think is his or her outlook?
8. In what ways would you alter your approach in order to better empathize with a young person, a person in crisis, a co-worker, etc.?
9. Do you tend to avoid weak, ineffective and inconsequential responses to the questions a client may ask or do you tend to respond by showing genuine understanding, support and concern?
10. When a person is in some life-threatening crisis (e.g., suicidal attempt, battering, or engaging in self-destructive violent behavior), are you careful not to condone such dangerous conduct? What would be an appropriate avenue of referral in such a case?

In communicating a solid sense of values in our way of handling individual cases, we most effectively help them.[3]

A Self-Evaluation of the Communication of Respect

Think about a recent situation when you gave care to someone. This unique person told you his/her story with its special humanness. Reflect on how you actually helped this individual through these questions. Share your thoughts in your journal, in pairs, small groups or in a large group discussion.

1. Are you pretentious and insincere, feigning friendship, in your relationships with your clients or do you relate to them as an equal in an intimate and sincere manner?
2. Do you care for each person as a unique human being?
3. Are you able to withhold your assessment of the convictions, tenets, feelings and conduct of other people? Do you try to press them into espousing your beliefs and norms of conduct?
4. Are you present to the other person in an unconditional, compassionate way?
5. Do you try to increase the effectiveness of the way you communicate with others?
6. Do you affirm other's natural gifts in order to help them appreciate and deal with their problems? Do you help people build on what they are saying and doing that seems to work for them?
7. Do you refrain from practices and conversation that favor your own interests? Are you comfortable not putting your agendas, assumptions and expectations on people?
8. Are you inclined to avoid jumping to conclusions, arriving at decisions or passing judgment on others until you have tried to walk for some time with them in their shoes?
9. Are you inclined to cherish the other as a person capable of thinking, expressing and doing what is best for him or her self?
10. Mindful of the need to always validate another by showing respect, are we at the same time cognizant of the special issues surrounding mental illness? How must our response vary depending on the severity of the person's condition? If the person needs specific psychological or therapeutic help, what referral avenues are available?

A Self-Evaluation of the Communication of Genuineness

How real are you with others? Are you always looking for just the "right" answer or "right response" from the person? How do you encourage people to choose their own path of love, healing and transformation? Reflect on the essential quality of genuineness with the following questions. Share what you learn in your journal, in pairs, small groups or in a large group discussion.

1. Are you spontaneous, sensitive and sincere with others or do you tend to be programmed, inflexible and somewhat hypocritical in your approach? Do you connect easily with those you are trying to help?
2. Are you willing to share yourself with your clients? Are you willing to risk being authentically open to them?
3. Do you deal with people and their families as a "trained expert" in a very learned manner using authoritative language or do you meet people where they are and seek to communicate with them as equals?
4. Are you able to avoid being thin-skinned and touchy when you are challenged?
5. Are you able to emphasize the positive and avoid negative, detrimental and unhealthy responses?
6. Are you predisposed to communicate even difficult matters in affirmative ways, opening up new areas of inquiry?
7. What are your personal therapeutic skills and competence? Have they helped you to assess correctly the emotional, physical, social and spiritual condition of those you serve? (Unless the pastoral care provider is a trained licensed clinician, he or she does not assume the responsibility of diagnosis or treatment of conditions that are beyond their scope and training. With other care professionals we embrace the commitment "to do no harm.")

A Self-Evaluation of the Communication of Warmth

Think about some recent situations in which you functioned as a caregiver. Reflect upon the quality of your warmth.

1. Do you communicate a spirit of warmth and approachability when you first meet others?
2. Do you communicate a sense of acceptance through your eyes and presence, concern, mindfulness and overall way of interacting with those to whom you offer care?
3. Are you mindful of attitudes and ways of communicating that may be interpreted as reprimanding or derogatory?
4. As you gain more practice and experience do you find it easier and more natural to converse with a significant measure of genuine warmth even with persons whom you've just met?

According to the research of Robert Carkhuff and Charles Truax, effective helpers are noted for their ability to communicate non-judgmental warmth, accurate empathy, and obvious genuineness.[4]

Pastoral and Spiritual Assessment

Caregivers are pastoral resource persons who help others discover and sort out personal values and meanings.[5] This perspective is becoming more common today even though the emphasis in much of this kind of care still remains on the biological and medical level[6] including psychiatric and psychological intervention. Though these clinical methods have importance, spiritual and pastoral caregivers provide a safe atmosphere for a person to peer into the mystery of his/her person, beyond medical, psychosocial and behavioral identifications and parameters. Articulating their sense of meaning, purpose, hope, love, forgiveness and concept of God help clients to identify the kind of support systems that can offer real assistance in their present situation.[7] We help them to articulate the extent that religious practices serve in bringing them strength in their present circumstances.[8]

Through a spiritual well-being inventory assessment, they are able to define what goals and values shape who they are. This resource is an instrument that helps clarify the core spiritual dimensions of life by determining the quality of one's satisfaction in prayer, an awareness of self-direction, comfort about the future and sense of well-being and happiness. This spiritual well-being resource functions as a measurement of a person's connectedness with life, self and God and in assessing the extent of their religious and existential well-being. Check this resource out as a tool for empowering people to deal with life[9] in all its fullness including death and dying.

Pastoral Resources for Death and Dying

At the hospital where I work, we explore the meaning of illness, dying and bereavement ministry through various pastoral education programs. This series includes a Pastoral Care and Counseling program for lay, clergy volunteers, and interested hospital staff. This is a year-long training program offered in weekly sessions. Now in its seventh year, many graduates of this pastoral adventure term it a life-changing endeavor. Two monthly ongoing pastoral education seminars for ministers, clergy and staff provide excellent opportunities for personal, ministerial, spiritual and theological reflection and growth. Participants come together in an atmosphere not unlike that of a supportive family. These pastoral education and training programs provide ministerial supervision and spiritual companionship. As a grief and bereavement minister, I recognize and discern more clearly the length, breadth, width and depth of God's love shining through the conversations, the insights, the passionate responses, the articulation of vulnerabilities, the expressions of faith that surface in sharing with my brothers and sisters. My spiritual and emotional caregiver colleagues share themselves with me and I am richer because of the encounter.

I recommend comparable pastoral education, support and mentor groups for ministering persons. We need places where pastoral persons can be ministered to and be with comrades in non-threatening and healthy environments. My experience points to our brokenness as 'the healers' who need healing. These pastoral resources unlock and amplify the 'good news' in our midst as our stories, theology, Scripture, thoughts and feelings are expressed in our gatherings.

There are other pastoral resources which provide opportunities for growth and healing. I refer to these videocassettes as worthwhile tools which help us come to grips vicariously with the dramatic issues of death and dying.

> *The Last Best Year,* starring Mary Tyler Moore and Bernadette Peters, narrates the life of a woman who is dying of cancer.[10]
>
> *Steel Magnolias,* starring Sally Field and Julia Roberts, portrays a vibrant young diabetic whose decision to have a baby costs her her life.[11]
>
> *Terms of Endearment,* starring Shirley MacLaine and Debra Winger, tells the story of a mother and daughter coping with cancer.[12]
>
> *Night Mother* stars Anne Bancroft and Sissy Spacek who are dealing with the reality of suicide.[13]
>
> *The Doctor* stars William Hurt, an insensitive physician who is changed by his own cancer experience.[14]
>
> Howard Clinebell's *Growing Through Loss*, is a video-cassette series of six sessions of a grief healing group and is useful training for facilitators on how to lead such groups.[15] A twelve video-cassette series, *Ministry to the Bereaved — Ministry in Times of Crisis*, covers the dy-

namics of loss/grief/bereavement with examples of various types of losses such as suicide, homicide and natural death.[16] It, too, is very useful.

Both role playing[17] and guided imagery exercises[18] are profitable tools helping caregivers to reflect on their style of ministry and evaluate their strengths and gifts as grief ministers. Through them they learn to critique their style of presence and methods of coping with grief, death and dying as they are forced to face their own shadow side in creative and healthy ways. This can be done in pairs, small groups and/or in large group discussion. Peer review of how one deals with issues of grief, death and dying can be highly profitable, engendering a greater sense of self-appropriation and appreciation of one's professional talents. Here are some issues for reflection:

1. How do you deal with another's grief?
2. How do you deal with your own losses (grief, death and dying)? Could you cope with them in a more effective way? The time used in reflecting on our history of personal loss pays high dividends in helping to make us more effective in our own work.[19]
3. Describe a situation in which you helped someone else deal with loss/grief, death and dying? Were you helpful or not? Explain.

Role Playing Exercise/Improv

Setting: an office in the church, hospital, school, etc.

Widowed Woman

A woman comes to a pastoral counselor to talk about her husband of 17 years who died a year and half ago from a heart attack. There were both good and difficult times in their marriage, but all and all she was happy. She hasn't been able to let go of him, although she had reluctantly taken off her wedding ring which reminded her of him. In the last year she has become more involved with the activities of her three children: a fourteen-year-old daughter, an eleven-year-old daughter and an eight-year-old son.

Sometimes she feels down for a few days at a time, not able to get on with life. She is wondering if her taking charge of everything during his dying and after might have something to do with her problem. Friends have told her that she has been so busy that maybe she didn't really fully grieve.

At a recent parish retreat, she met a pastoral counselor. In the improv, portray the scene when she has decided to talk with the pastoral counselor in hopes of sorting out where she is with her grief, her life and to discern what God is saying to her.

Pastoral Counselor

The pastoral counselor has a meeting with this woman who wants to talk about trying to get back into life, to explore what God is saying to her. The caregiver met the woman at a recent church retreat where she assisted as a team member and spiritual companion/director.[20]

Reflections on the Improv

After improvising this role playing, discuss what you did as pastoral caregiver. Share your learnings in pairs, small groups and/or in large group discussion. Write them in your journal.

Affirm your strengths and discuss what you would do differently or change in your way of responding the next time. Reflect on what was going on inside of you as gave care. Articulate images and models of ministry presence which framed the way your handled yourself with this person.

1. What was the most important thing you gave to this grieving woman?
2. What did she want from you as a caregiver?
3. Describe what pastoral grief caregiving skills (e.g., listening, empathy, genuineness, etc.) were entailed in this situation?
4. What would you change in your presence and/or way of listening and responding to this woman? Is your approach limited to the medical, clinical, administrative, ecclesial or academic or is it more "human"?[21]

Reflection Monologue

As you listen to this woman's thoughts, put yourself in the role of a pastoral grief minister desiring to communicate a compassionate presence to her. Share your feelings, insights and concerns.

Setting: a room in a hospice center or a convalescent hospital.

The following is improvised as a dramatic reading of a dying woman speaking about her fears, needs and feelings to grief ministers.

Woman

"I lay here in bed and wonder if you notice my pain. I wish you would reach out to me. Don't be put off by my calm exterior, by my seeming control. I need your care and concern. I want to know I'm O.K. I need you to let me know I can talk about my dying. I bet you'd like to run away and avoid me. So would I! I am scared, and I'm the one who's dying! I need your presence so I won't feel so alone.

"Please don't desert me. I am asking you to touch my fears that I hide so well. I need you as a friend. I bet you're probably scared to get too close. If you share a part of yourself with me, you'll receive something from me, and a piece of you will die when I die.

"Yet, if you are with me as a caring friend, you'll make a difference in my life. You'll help me know that I belong and am worthwhile even in death."

Reflection on the Monologue

After listening to this woman's grief in this dramatic reading jot down your reflections in your journal. If you are with others (in pairs, or in large or small groups) discuss the following:

1. As you hear the dying woman's thoughts, what was your experience?
2. How would you minister to this woman?
3. What does she ask of her caregiver?
5. What kind of presence would you offer to this person?

Guided Imagery Exercise

Guided imagery exercises are opportunities for us, through the vehicle of the imagination, to move through situations of grief. As we enter into these exercises our actual physiological responses change. Muscle tension, size of pupils, heart rate, respiration and blood glucose levels,[22] are all altered as the images we conjure up connect with the synapses of our brain and are transmitted through our nerves and biochemical processes. New feelings emerge from the depths of our soul and lingering memories integrate past wounds of our psyche and spirit. These images, insights and feelings influence our physiology.

Guided imagery exercises are not magic formulae for fixing everything, but they are a helpful pastoral resource when used in a (w)holistic approach to healing, growth and spiritual transformation. The following guided imagery exercise is a way to visualize and personally experience your own dying process and death. If your are alone, record the exercise on a cassette tape. Then play it back listening to your recording. If you are with others, either record the exercise on a cassette tape or have someone act as leader and read the guided imagery exercise. Get in a comfortable place. Close your eyes. Take a few deep breaths and relax.

Guided Imagery Exercise: Your Death

Setting: a doctor's office.

You have just been told you have a few months to live. Your cancer has spread through your whole body, through all your organs and tissues. The physician says there is no treatment. There is nothing that can be done.

What are you feeling and thinking? Let these thoughts and feelings surface. Allow them to well up from deep within you. Take some time and just be with yourself.

What are your initial reactions and sensations? Sit with any moods or images that you are aware of right now. Just sense these initial reactions from the medical news just received.

Briefly open your eyes and write down any phrases or words that come to mind. Just jot down a few brief impressions of what is going on inside of you. Take a couple of minutes to do this. When you have recorded a few impressions and feelings, then close your eyes again.

Who do you want to talk to about your impending death? Visualize that person before you now. Go wherever you like to be with this person. What do you want to say? Let the images and sensations surface? What are you thinking? What are you feeling?

Spend a few minutes saying what you need to say to this person.

Briefly open your eyes and write down what you said to this person, and how you spent your time together. Jot down your thoughts and conversation. Take 5 minutes or so to do this. When you have finished writing your thoughts and feelings about this conversation, once again close your eyes.

Are there any other persons you want to talk to about your death? Visualize these persons too. Spend some time with them. What are you saying to them? What do you want from them?

In your last few months of life, what do you want to do? Who do you want to connect with during this time? How are you planning to spend these days? Take some time to watch these last few months enfold before you. Spend a few minutes in silence as you consider what you are doing with your life. Pause for 3-5 minutes.

Open your eyes again and write down what you experienced. Take 3-5 minutes for this writing exercise. When you are finished, once again close you eyes.

You become aware of the gradual deterioration in your health. The disease has now taken its toll on you. You know you are dying and won't be in this world too much longer. Use your imagination and see or sense how you want to die. Are you at a hospital, hospice house or your own home? What kind of comfort treatment measures do you want?

Who is taking care of you now? What individuals are here with you now? Are you holding on to any spiritual supports? Is prayer something important to you at this time? What kind of prayer do you want? Do you want any spiritual ministers or caregivers to be with you now? Do you have any requests for your funeral arrangements and ceremony? Is there anything else you want?

Now see yourself dying. You are taking your last breaths on this earth. All consciousness of your body is fading away. Sense yourself leaving this life and embarking on another. What is it like? What are your perceptions? How do you feel about yourself in this spiritual dimension? What do you think about your life beyond death? What is it like? Spend some time in your new home. Savor the images and sensations. Take a few minutes of silence to soak in this experience. Pause for 3-5 minutes.

When you are ready, open your eyes and write down your dying and "life after death" experiences. Allow these to be expressed effortlessly as they flow from your pen. Let your dying and new life experiences gel into whatever story or form that emerges. Take about 15-25 minutes for this writing exercise.[23]

After you have completed your writing you may wish to share some of this experience with others.

If you are with others, discuss your insights in pairs, in small groups or in a large group discussion. Share only what you choose to talk about. You may choose not to talk about your experience. We want to respect the sacredness of each individual by allowing each person to discuss only what he or she feels comfortable doing.

Personal Reflections on Issues Concerning Death

When we are honest with ourselves and others about the implications of the dying process, we gain personal insights which will be helpful to us when we assist others who are facing death.[24] A very useful pastoral resource is the appropriate of use of Scripture as an aid in the mourning experience. The psalms are particularly meaningful to those who are experiencing grief.[25] Bereavement ministers offer spiritual care through the development of the appropriate use of the sacraments, prayer, Scripture and other religious resources.[26]

Another pastoral resource in the dying process is the recognition of our motivations and expectations surrounding death. An awareness of personal defenses frees the spiritual caregiver to journey with people in the process of their dying.[27] Personal reflection — of one's religious and spiritual issues, assumptions and expectations about death and dying — unlocks a passage for inner healing and greater effectiveness in one's ministry with others.

1. What do want to do for the dying person? What pastoral duties do you want to perform?
2. Be mindful of your affective state. Notice your feelings.
3. Put yourself in the dying person's position. What is that like for you?
4. Offer your pastoral presence to the person and family members.
5. Try not to get caught up in agendas (e.g., to be a problem solver, messiah, teacher, cheerleader, 'the expert,' etc.). Agendas tend to stifle what God desires to do.
6. Respect the dying person's need for respite, quiet or for special people to be close at hand.[28]

Reflect on this material and evaluate how you deal with issues surrounding death and dying. Write down your insights in a journal. If you are with others, discuss what you have learned.

Appendix B

REFLECTIONS ON CARING FOR THE DYING

This section deals with reflections on caring for the dying. It helps to bring into focus some of the issues a caregiver may experience in caring for someone who is dying. Our continued personal self-reflection and sharing with others energizes us to offer effective care to ourselves and other people. As we help ourselves cope with death, we have greater sensitivity, acceptance and discernment about this unique mystery.

1. What am I *feeling* when ministering to individuals who are dying?
2. What am I *thinking* when ministering to individuals who are dying?
3. What do I *say* to a person who is dying?
4. Is it tedious or effortless to converse with someone who is dying? What is the most perplexing thing for me when I am dealing with a person who is dying?
5. What qualms or misgivings do I have as I minister to a dying person? Are there doubts or matters I would rather not be confronted with by the dying person?
6. Do I have any musings or unrest about my own death and dying?
7. What are my presuppositions and agendas when I serve as a pastoral grief caregiver to a dying person?
8. With only three months left to live, what would I be most concerned about?

9. If my death were approaching soon, what would I be doing during this final phase of my life?
10. Have I accomplished everything I have wanted to realize with my life? Do I have any remorse? What else do I need to take care of or do before I die?

Appendix C

RESOURCES FOR CAREGIVERS

A Pastoral Care Training Program is a valuable asset in developing spiritual persons who effectively minister to others in hospitals, churches, schools and in other settings. The following story and meditation illustrate how a skilled Pastoral Care Volunteer in her patient visitation is able to integrate the spiritual and emotional dimensions of (w)holistic care. This pastoral interaction takes place in a healthcare facility, but it could happen in any number of ministerial settings.

Resources: Pastoral Care Volunteers

It was 2:00 p.m. when Mary came to work. She walked into the Pastoral Care Department at the hospital and was greeted by the two staff chaplains on duty. Mary signed in and picked up her room assignments for patient visitation. After putting on her photo I.D. badge, she went up to the Surgical Floor. As she walked off the elevator she saw Donna, an R.N. on this floor. Donna had come to trust Mary's skills as a caring listener during her last six months visiting patients on the floor. Mary had developed a reputation as someone with whom patients enjoyed sharing their stories and needs in an atmosphere of acceptance and warmth.

Donna said, "Please visit Mrs. Jones; she had surgery yesterday and was a little teary earlier." Mary thanked Donna for telling her about the patient's need. She went to the room and found Mrs. Jones sitting quietly, obviously preoccupied about something.

After the initial introductions, Mrs. Jones related some of the details of her surgery. She gradually began to talk about her real concerns. She was a single mother who had been out of work for several months and was raising two children. The doctor told her she had to have this surgery right away to remove her gall bladder. Mrs. Jones was concerned about how she would pay the hospital bill and take care of her small children during this period. This surgery set her back because she was unable to look for a job at this time.

As Mrs. Jones talked about her situation, Mary listened attentively to her difficulties. It seems that she had done secretarial work in the past but had lost her position through some recent down-sizing at her place of employment. She expressed her fear of the future, not knowing what would transpire. She also felt very much alone because her family lived out of state. In the course of her story she mentioned going to the local Presbyterian church where she felt comfortable. Mary knew that this church was very active in assisting their parishioners in need and asked if she wanted someone from the church to see her. Mrs. Jones expressed her openness in having someone from the church talk to her.

Mary set up the meeting with a church representative who discussed with Mrs. Jones the possibility of cutting costs through living with a roommate. Another single mother with one child wanted to share rent and utilities with a Christian woman. Mrs. Jones agreed to the idea. They would live together, share costs and help one another. Catholic Social Services was contacted to help provide some groceries for Mrs. Jones while she was out of work.

One of the staff chaplains followed up on Mary's visit and a medical social worker was brought into the situation. Mrs. Jones expressed her gratitude to the nursing staff for the Pastoral Care

Volunteer's compassionate assistance. Most of her concerns were taken care of by the time she left the hospital. There was even a temporary typing position found by a church member which Mrs. Jones could do from her home while recuperating.

This example of the effectiveness of Pastoral Care Volunteers could be multiplied over and over again. These volunteers generally train for a year, meeting once a week, as they hone their pastoral skills. It is a resource no healthcare facility should overlook.

Meditation on the Source Within[1]

The following guided meditation was used with patients, students, spiritual directees, retreatants, friends and other seekers.

> As we begin this healing journey... all that is needed is a willing heart... a comfortable place... where you can relax... loosen your clothing... close your eyes. Breathe deeply... follow your breath... deeply... filling the lungs.... Breathe in love... breathe out peace.
>
> Be aware of any noise around you... and be aware of the sounds inside of you. Continue to breathe deeply... feeling the energy of life fill your being... feel the flow of the source within.
>
> We place ourselves in the presence of God... into the heart of our life... to hear... sense... and feel every aspect of who we are.
>
> Like a wave gently washing across your whole body, this life energy... has calmed and soothed... every cell, muscle and bone... All is in balance... calm... connected... at peace.
>
> Oh Divine Healer, Spirit of Love for all your children, we ask for your healing touch... your life energy.

Let any healing treatments that you are working through: radiation..., chemotherapy..., surgery..., psychological counseling... or spiritual direction, prayer, nutrition, learning, friendship, love... pass through the power, love and warmth of this healing Light.

Now see that your therapeutic process and treatments are coming from this healing Light — who is Jesus Christ, the Light of the World — your Light.

We invite you, Being of Light, to enter, touch and heal every part of our body, mind and spirit. As we look inside our body, we will look for healing... for the elimination of all disease.

Watch and welcome this loving Light enter your blood stream. Your blood stream flows throughout your entire system vibrating with this Light... health. Like a river of life, cleansing, healing, nourishing your cells, the energy of life surges through your system.

Viruses, weak or diseased cells, tumors can all be destroyed by the Light as it radiates warmth and healing. See this in your mind's eye. Each cell of your immune system is handmade by God, strengthened by the power of His Light.... Imagine it flushing out the waste products of these dissolved weakened cells. Toxins are safely removed from your body.

The Light floods the organs of the body... strengthening and healing every part of your being. All the glory of God is celebrated in the wisdom of your body.

See yourself healthy, alive and fully healed. Picture yourself well... healthy with all your life energy... pulsating in Jesus' healing light. Stay here as long as you need until you are ready to come back to your surroundings.

Think of God's energy and radiating Light staying with you as you leave this meditation and return to your everyday surroundings.[2]

* * * * *

If you are interested in buying an audio-cassette of the *Meditation on the Source Within*, write Anmchara Cruces, Inc., P.O. Box 1172, Bend, Oregon 97709.

For information on setting up workshops and dramatic ministry presentations for pastoral training programs, Scripture classes, etc. and retreats for spiritual growth and transformation tailored to your community's needs at your church, hospital, school, etc., contact Dr. Jerry Roussell, Jr., D. Min., Anmchara Cruces, Inc., P.O. Box 1172, Bend, Oregon 97709 [Phone: (541) 385-7431].

* * * * *

It has been a privilege to share *Dealing With Grief, Theirs and Ours* with you. It is my hope that the readings and reflections in this book have been helpful to you as a pastoral resource both personally and ministerially. May you be blessed abundantly in your endeavors and may the reign of God be with you now and forever. Amen.

Appendix D

ANNOTATED BIBLIOGRAPHY ON PASTORAL RESOURCE LITERATURE

An annotated bibliography on pastoral literature is an invaluable resource for spiritual and emotional caregivers. This resource material is for personal and professional growth. A list of useful resources for pastoral ministers follows:

Arnold, Joan Hagan and Penelope Buschman Gemma. *A Child Dies— A Portrait of Family Grief.* Rockville, MD: Aspen Publication, 1983.

This book discusses the changes people go through after the loss of a child. The authors discuss the devastation of parents and their search for meaning when a child dies.

Augsburger, David. *Pastoral Counseling Across Cultures.* Philadelphia: The Westminster Press, 1986.

The author looks at the process of care from a cross-cultural perspective. This work moves through theology of family, culture, values, etc.

Bausch, William. *Ministry: Traditions, Tensions, Traditions.* Mystic, CT: Twenty-Third Publications, 1982.

This work covers the development of ministry from the early Church through the present day. This book addresses the (w)holistic care of the sick as part of the Church's ministry.

Brister, C.W. *Pastoral Care in the Church.* New York: Harper and Row, Publishers, 1964.

This classic work describes the pastoral care ministry. It

focuses on dimensions of the pastor's concern within the life of the Church.

Browning, Don. *Religious Thought and the Modern Psychologies: A Critical Conversation in the Theology of Culture*. Philadelphia: Fortress Press, 1987.

The scholarly work critiques modern psychologies as purveyors of culture. Topics include vision and obligation in Christian anthropology, self-actualization and harmony in humanistic psychology, generativity and care in Erikson and Kohut, etc.

Cavanagh, Michael. *The Effective Minister*. San Francisco: Harper and Row, Publishers, 1975.

The author discusses issues necessary for pastors to be effective ministers. Topics include growth, difficulties and pitfalls, pastoral identity and spirituality, etc.

Clements, William. *Care and Counseling of the Aging*. Philadelphia: Fortress Press, 1979.

The author provides a creative synthesis of psychological and theological insights. This book expands on perspectives about aging along with some practical and theoretical insights into the often unrealized potential of this time of life.

Davis, Martha, Elizabeth Robbins, and Matthew McKay. *The Relaxation and Stress Reduction Workbook*. Richmond, CA: New Harbinger Publications, 1980.

This work provides both information and exercises in guided imagery, relaxation, etc. It is a useful pastoral resource offering a variety of behavioral tools.

Egan, Gerard. *The Skilled Helper: A Systematic Approach to Effective Helping*, 3d ed. Monterey, CA: Brooks/Cole Publishing Company, 1986.

The author develops a systematic approach for counseling theory and skills. This book describes the helping model, stages of counseling, and integration of skills with clients.

Fath, Gerald. *Health Care Ministries: Organization/Management/ Evaluation*. St. Louis, MO: The Catholic Health Association of the United States, 1983.

This work focuses on pastoral care ministry in healthcare settings. This book develops a systematic way to set-up and evaluate a pastoral care program in a Catholic healthcare facility.

Figley, Charles R. and Hamilton McCubbin, ed. *Stress and the Family. Volume I: Coping with Normative Transitions.* New York: Brunner/Mazel, Inc., 1983.

This volume is given over to coping with stressors in the family that are normative (parenthood, dual-career families, divorce, step-parenting, single parenting, societal stress, environmental stress, economic stress, etc.). It deals with family adaptation and coping with loss from a sociological research perspective.

Figley, Charles R. and Hamilton McCubbin, ed. *Stress and the Family. Volume II: Coping with Catastrophe.* New York: Brunner/Mazel, Inc., 1983.

This volume is given over to coping with stressors in the family that are catastrophic (chronic illness and family stress, drug abuse, abandonment, unemployment, rape, captivity, disaster, war, etc.). It deals with family adaptation and coping with loss from a sociological research perspective.

Fortune, Marie. *Is Nothing Sacred? The Story of a Pastor, The Women He Sexually Abused, and The Congregation He Nearly Destroyed.* San Francisco: Harper Collins Publishers, 1989.

This work relates the personal stories of several women who have been sexually abused by their pastor and their loss of a sense of the sacred and the image of the parish community as a safe place.

Harbaugh, Gary. *Pastor as Person: Maintaining Personal Integrity in the Choices and Challenges of Ministry.* Minneapolis: Augsburg Publishing House, 1984.

This work uses a biblical (w)holistic model to address the spiritual dimension at the center of human experience. This (w)holistic model integrates the physical, emotional, mental, and social dimensions of the person together with one's history and choices.

Haylor, Haylor. "Human Practitioner," *Nurse Practitioner* 12, no. 5 (May 1987): 64.

This article looks at how triggering episodes of loss experienced in the present remind us of earlier losses.

Hiltner, Seward. *Preface to Pastoral Theology*. New York: Abingdon Press, 1958.

This classic work describes pastoral care ministry. This book discusses pastoral theology through the perspective of shepherding including its healing, sustaining, and guiding aspects.

Joesten, Leroy. "The Voices of the Dying and the Bereaved: A Bridge Between Loss and Growth," in *Hospital Ministry: The Role of the Chaplain Today*, ed. Lawrence Holst. New York: Crossroad Publications, 1985.

The author describes how pastoral care givers walk with people in the struggle between valuing the acceptance of death, yet resisting it at the same time.

Kübler-Ross, Elisabeth. *Death: The Final Stage of Growth*. Englewood Cliffs, NJ: Prentice-Hall, Inc., 1975.

This work develops the theme that all the endeavors and actions of a person's life culminate in death.

Linn, Dennis, Matthew Linn and Sheila Fabricant. "Healing Relationships with Miscarried, Aborted, and Stillborn Babies," *Journal of Christian Healing* 7, no. 2 (1985): 30-40.

This article deals with healing after the loss of a baby.

Linn, Mary, Dennis Linn, and Matthew Linn. *Healing the Dying: Releasing People to Die*. New York: Paulist Press, 1979.

The theme of how to help a person be healed and whole in their dying is covered in this book.

Miller, Jerome. *The Way of Suffering: A Geography of Crisis*. Washington, DC: Georgetown University Press, 1988.

This book elaborates on the theme of spiritual suffering which calls an individual to surrender control and self-centeredness in the crisis of suffering.

Montague, George. *Building Christ's Body: The Dynamics of Christian Living According to St. Paul*, Herald Scriptural Library. ed. Robert Karris. Chicago, IL: Franciscan Herald Press, 1975.

The author uses the body of Christ image as his theme throughout this work. Topics include the Spirit and the body, Christ, the Mystery of God, etc.

Niklas, Gerald. *The Making of a Pastoral Person.* 2nd Revised Edition. New York: Alba House, 1996.

This work covers the process of care through knowing oneself and using it to enhance one's ministry. Topics include pastoral identity, feelings, spirituality, etc.

Niklas, Gerald and Charlotte Stefanics. *Ministry to the Sick.* New York: Alba House, 1982.

The authors describe ministry to those who are sick and dying. This work includes discussion of pastoral sacramental care.

Rosenthal, H.R. "The Fear of Death as an Indispensable Factor in Psychotherapy," *American Journal of Psychotherapy* 17 (1963): 629.

This article describes the diverse ways people deal with their fear of death. People play down or repress the issue. Some anesthetize the pain and avoid talking about the issue. Others refuse to think about death or think about it all the time.

Seidl, Lawrence. "When the Bough Breaks: Pastoral Care for Families of Dying Infants," *Health Progress* (September 1989): 50-51.

This article talks about how pastoral persons walk a fine line between medical staff, family, and other clergy.

Whitehead, James and Evelyn Whitehead. *Method in Ministry: Theological Reflection and Christian Ministry.* New York: The Seabury Press, 1983.

This ministry work details a model of theological reflection based on drawing together tradition, cultural information, and personal experience to deal with a pastoral concern. Through listening, asserting, and deciding, the authors develop an interactive method which weaves together these three diverse poles of sources.

Appendix E

ANNOTATED BIBLIOGRAPHY ON GRIEF LITERATURE

A descriptive annotated bibliography on grief literature is an invaluable pastoral resource for spiritual and emotional caregivers. This resource material is for personal and professional growth. A list of useful resources for grief ministers follows:

Bozarth, A.R. *A Journey through Grief.* Minneapolis, MN: CompCare Publishers, 1990.

This gentle book employs short essays and poems for the difficult grief stages offering help in mourning.

Colgrove, Melba et al. *How to Survive the Loss of a Love: 58 Things to do When There is Nothing to be Done*. Toronto, New York: Bantam Books, 1977.

This work lists the stages of recovery as shock/denial, anger/depression, and understanding/acceptance. This helpful work outlines practical ways to make it through the process of losing a loved one.

Crenshaw, D.A. *Bereavement: Counseling the Grieving Throughout the Life Cycle.* New York: Continuum, 1990.

Both professional and lay caregivers help people through the tasks of grieving, and provide guidelines to help preschool age children, adolescents, young adults, and the elderly resolve their issues.

Detrick, Richard, and Nicola Steele. *How to Recover from Grief.* Valley Forge, PA: Judson Press, 1983.

This work outlines practical ways to respond and express

personal grief. Chapters focus on the stages of grief, anger, guilt, normal/abnormal grief, and help of self and others.

Donnelley, N.H. *I Never Know What to Say: How to Help your Family and Friends Cope with Tragedy*. New York: Ballantine Books, 1987.

A Protestant chaplain describes her own and others' experiences, offering guidance about how to help with grief. When do you talk? When do you keep silent? When do you offer practical help? How can your friend reconcile shattering loss with the concept of an all-loving God?

Engel, George. "Grief and Grieving," *American Journal of Nursing* 64, no. 9 (1964).

This article covers both the theory and practical problems of grief. It describes normal grieving and suggests ways to help the grief-stricken.

Engel, G.L. "Is Grief a Disease?" *Psychological Medicine* 23 (1961): 18-23.

Through interviews and observations with chronically ill individuals, Engel studies patients' reactions to loss within the medical setting. The author defines the characteristics of the grieving process and its outcome.

Grollman, E.A. *Living When a Loved One has Died*. Boston: Beacon Press, 1977.

This collection of poems and photos organizes grief into four areas: shock, suffering, recovery, and new life. This work offers understanding and reassurance to the reader.

Hopson, B., and J. Adams. "Toward an Understanding of Transition: Defining Some Boundaries of Transition," in *Human Adaptations: Coping with Crisis*, ed. R. Moss. Lexington, MA: Health, 1977.

This work develops a model of change which encompasses the period leading up to adult transition.

Johnson, S.E. *After a Child Dies: Counseling Bereaved Families*. New York: Springer Publishing Company, 1987.

Drawing upon the author's work with bereaved families, this book focuses on the experience of a child's death. It addresses a child's concept of death, family issues in coping with death, and grief symptoms. This work delineates the first, second, and third years of bereavement along with professional intervention.

Krauss, P., and M. Goldfisher. *Why Me? Coping with Grief, Loss and Change.* New York: Bantam Books, 1981.

One author, a Jewish chaplain at Sloan-Kettering Cancer Center, draws on personal experiences of tragedy. The work deals with how to talk about loss and grief in the midst of crisis and how to cope using hope as opportunity for personal growth and wholeness.

Kushner, H.S. *When Bad Things Happen to Good People.* New York: Schocken Books, 1981.

A rabbi relates the tragedy of losing his 14-year-old son to progeria (a rapid aging disease), forcing him to rethink everything he had been taught about God and God's ways. The author writes for people who have been hurt by life and wonder about God and justice. He writes for people who are angry at God or want to know where to turn for strength and hope.

Lindemann, Erich. *Beyond Grief: Studies in Crisis Intervention.* New York: Jason Aronsonn, 1979.

This study reviews the correlation between the loss of a part of the body and neurosis or depression, between a life situation and mental status in the disease process. It argues the need for the availability of professional services for those in grief crisis. This study explores the symptomatology and management of acute grief and reactions to fatal illness in the health care arena.

———. "Symptomatology and Management of Acute Grief," *American Journal of Psychiatry* 101 (1944): 141-148.

This classic work studies the grief process for 101 survivors, their relatives, and those who lost a loved one in the Cocoanut Grove fire of 1942. The study discusses psychological and somatic symptomatology including the appearance of delayed, or exaggerated/absent grief experiences, and the movement from distorted into normal grief and its resolution.

Marris, P. *Loss and Change.* New York: Pantheon Books, 1974.

This Pulitzer Prize-winning work develops a theoretical

understanding of mourning through querying the losses of widows and slum clearance.

Melges, Frederick T. *Time and the Inner Future: A Temporal Approach to Psychiatric Disorders*. New York: John Wiley and Sons, 1982.

Time affects various experiences of loss. Melges evaluates the effect of time on emotional dysfunctions. The grief process reaches resolution through the use of current clinical practice.

Moustakas, C. *Loneliness*. Englewood Cliffs, NJ: Prentice-Hall, Inc., 1962.

_______. *Loneliness and Love*. Englewood Cliffs, NJ: Prentice-Hall, Inc., 1972.

_______. *Turning Point*. Englewood Cliffs, NJ: Prentice-Hall, Inc., 1977.

This author journeys through life crises which include loss, the threat of loss, and death.

Oates, Wayne. *Your Particular Grief*. Philadelphia: The Westminster Press, 1981.

This book talks about grief from the personal dimension of the one experiencing it. This work explores anticipatory, traumatic, no-end, and near-miss grief. The author deals with how to grieve and how to get well even when facing issues of powerlessness, as well as meaning.

Parkes, Colin Murray. *Bereavement: Studies of Grief in Adult Life*. Madison, CT: International Universities Press, Inc., 1987.

This work discusses grief from a psychoanalytic/psychodynamic point of view. It describes how a significant loss can affect trust, resulting in an avoidance of human involvement. This study portrays the alarm reaction of bereavement as being similar to the characteristics of the fight/flight syndrome. Chapters include determinants of grief, the broken heart, searching, mitigation, and organizations which can be helpful for the bereaved.

_______. "Psychological Care of the Family after the Patient's Death," in *Acute Grief*, ed. P. Margolis et al. New York: Columbia University Press, 1981.

_______. "The First Year of Bereavement," *Psychiatry* 33 (1968): 444-467.

These studies look at those who have lost a loved one such as widows and widowers. This research distinguishes between uncomplicated grief responses and complicated grief reactions (chronic, inhibited, and delayed).

Ramsay, R.W. "Behavioral Approaches to Bereavement," *Behavioral Respiratory Therapy* 15 (1977): 131-135.

Bereavement is examined by scrutinizing widows, parents, and family/friends of a suicide victim. A stage theory for pathologic grief reactions is developed.

Rosenblatt, Paul C. *Bitter, Bitter Tears: Nineteenth-Century Diarists and Twentieth-Century Grief Theories.* Minneapolis, MN: University of Minnesota Press, 1983.

Rosenblatt studies various themes of grief through using 19th-century diarists. This research includes the resistance of family systems to change after loss and the contrasts in the loss experience of those left behind and the 'leavers.' The author focuses on issues of emotional control, discontinuity, struggle, and retreat.

Schlossberg, N.K. "A Model for Analyzing Human Adaptation to Transition," *Counseling Psychology* 9 (1981): 2-18.

This author postulates a theory of loss related to adult transitions.

Schoenberg, B. et al. *Loss and Grief.* New York: Columbia University Press, 1970.

This study by the Columbia University Thanatology Group researches loss and grief in the psychosocial management of medical patients.

Simpson, S. *The Survivor's Guide: Coping with the Details of Death.* Toronto: Summerhill Press, 1990.

This helpful workbook explains how to make it through the practical, legal, and financial decisions after someone dies. It describes steps to take within the first few hours and days; suggest what to do after the service; and functions as a "tool kit" with forms, lists of questions, etc.

Switzer, David. *The Dynamics of Grief.* Nashville, TN: Abingdon Press, 1970.

This work describes grief as an acute attack of anxiety precipitated by an external event such as the death of an intimate loved one. The author presents an overview of key studies in the literature of grief.

Temes, Roberta. *Living with an Empty Chair: A Guide Through Grief.* New York: Irvington Publishers, Inc., 1984.

The author uses a touching style and very human approach to work through grief. This work speaks to professionals and those who mourn. Suggestions are given on how to manage the stages of grief. Chapters discuss living alone, restructuring families, exploring children's reactions, and rebuilding one's life. Illustrations are dispersed throughout which bring comfort to the reader.

Westberg, Granger. *Good Grief: A Constructive Approach to Problems of Loss.* Philadelphia: Fortress Press, 1973.

This classic work views grief from a religious perspective. It is well worth the reader's time.

NOTES

Chapter 1

[1] Coval B. MacDonald, "Loss and Bereavement," in *Clinical Handbook of Pastoral Counseling*, eds. Robert Wicks, Richard Parsons, and Donald Capps (New York: Paulist Press, 1984), 544; and Kenneth R. Mitchell and Herbert Anderson, *All Our Losses, All Our Griefs— Resources for Pastoral Care* (Philadelphia: Westminster Press, 1983), 110.

[2] *Ibid.*

[3] Bette Midler and Barbara Hershey, *Beaches*, produced by Terri Schwartz, 123 minutes, Touchstone Pictures, 1988, videocassette.

[4] *Ibid.*

[5] Gerald R. Niklas and Charlotte Stefanics, *Ministry to the Sick* (New York: Alba House, 1982), 13.

[6] Clinebell, Howard. *Basic Types of Pastoral Counseling: Resources for the Ministry of Healing and Growth, Completely Revised and Enlarged* (Nashville, TN: Abingdon Press, 1984), 49-50.

[7] *Ibid.*, 50.

[8] Donald Capps, *Pastoral Care and Hermeneutics* (Philadelphia: Fortress Press, 1984), 50. For further in diagnostic assessment and pastoral action see the following works. Paul W. Pruyser, *The Minister as Diagnostician* (Philadelphia: Westminster Press, 1984), 14-134; Clinebell, Howard. *op. cit.*, 49-50; William B. Oglesby, Jr., *Biblical Themes for Pastoral Care and Counseling* (Nashville, TN: Abingdon Press, 1980), 13-44.

Various approaches to healing through the use of both psychology and theology are displayed with a pastoral perspective. (Robert J. Wicks, Richard D. Parsons, and Donald Capps, eds., *Clinical Handbook of Pastoral Counseling* [New York: Integration Books, 1985], 5-558; John Sanford, *Healing and Wholeness* [New York: Paulist Press, 1966], 5-157; Morton Kelsey, *Psychology, Medicine and Christian Healing* [New York: Harper and Row, 1966], 1-335).

[9] Clinebell, 67.

[10] *Ibid.*, 67.

[11] Julia Roberts and Campbell Scott, *Dying Young*, produced by Sally Field and Kevin McCormick, 111 minutes, Twentieth Century Fox, 1991, videocassette.

[12] *Ibid.*

[13] Edgar N. Jackson, "Why You Should Understand Grief: A Minister's Views," in *Resources for Ministry in Death and Dying*, eds. Larry Platt and Roger Branch (Nashville, TN: Broadman Press, 1988), 222.

[14] Rituals and ceremonies serve as a way to express those deeply embedded feelings and inner yearnings too intense to be put into words. Edgar N. Jackson, "Why You Should Understand Grief: A Minister's Views," in *Resources for Ministry in Death and Dying*, 222.

The need and significance of ritual are detailed in the following works: R. Scott Sullender, *Grief and Growth: Pastoral Resources for Emotional and Spiritual Growth* (New York: Paulist Press, 1985), 144-167; J. Gallen, "The Necessity of Ritual," *The Way* 13 (1973): 27-282; R. Pannikar, "Man as a Ritual Being," *Chicago Studies* 16 (1977): 5-28.

[15] Richard Kalish defines denial as an unconscious defense mechanism in which certain thoughts, feelings, or wishes are disavowed because of their painful or threatening nature· Richard A. Kalish, *Death, Grief, and Caring Relationships* (Monterey, CA: Brooks/Cole Publishing Company, 1985), 76.

[16] *Ibid.*, 86. Fear of death and life are discussed in *The Art of Dying*. Robert E. Neale, *The Art of Dying* (New York: Harper and Row, 1973), 24-48.

[17] H. Feifel and A.B. Branscomb, "Who's Afraid of Death?" *Journal of Abnormal Psychology* 81, 9 (1973): 282-288.

[18] Liston O. Mills, ed., *Perspectives on Death* (Nashville and New York: Abingdon Press, 1969), 201.

[19] Kalish, 189. Ways to cope with the fears of death of death are discussed in *Getting Well Again*. O.C. Simonton, Stephanie Matthews Simonton, and James Creighton, *Getting Well Again* (New York: Bantam Books, 1978), 228-240.

[20] Alan Deuel, "The Implications of Death Anxiety in the Writings of Becker, Lifton, and Yalom for an Adult Education Approach to Dying and Death" (D.Min. diss., San Francisco Theological Seminary, 1985), 62.

[21] C.S. Hall and G. Lindzey, *Theories of Personality*, 2d ed. (New York: John Wiley and Sons, Inc., 1970), 47. Transference is another denial defense mechanism. (Alan Deuel, "The Implications of Death Anxiety in the Writings of Becker, Lifton, and Yalom for an Adult Education Approach to Dying and Death" [D.Min. diss., San Francisco Theological Seminary, 1985], 97-98).

Examples of defense mechanisms are repression, displacement, reaction formation and sublimation. (C.S. Hall and G. Lindzey, *Theories of Personality*, 2d ed. [New York: John Wiley and Sons, Inc., 1970], 47, 49.)

[22] Rosemary Radford Ruether, *Sexism and God-Talk: Toward A Feminist Theology* (Boston: Beacon Press, 1983), 236.

[23] Ruether, 236; and Jeanne Achterberg, *Woman as Healer* (Boston: Shambhala, 1990), 203-204.

[24] Ernest Becker, *Denial of Death* (New York: Free Press, 1973), 168.

[25] Robert Bellah, *Habits of the Heart: Individualism and Commitment in American Life* (San Francisco: Harper Collins, 1986), 1-384.

[26] *Ibid.*, 168-169.

[27] Alfred Adler, *The Practice and Theory of Individual Psychology* (London: Kegan Paul, 1924), chapter 21, quoted in, Ernest Becker, *Denial of Death*, 210. Illustrations are cited from American culture which indicate the difficulty of people accepting death as part of the life cycle. (Robert Lifton and Eric Olson, *Living and Dying* [New York: Praeger Publishers, Inc., 1974], 34-35).

[28] Becker, 216. See these references for further contemporary comments on women having to conform to idealized notions of perfect bodies. (Naomi Wolf, *The Beauty Myth — How Images of Beauty are used against Women* [New York: Anchor/ Doubleday, 1991], 9-291; and Susan Brownmiller, *Femininity* [New York: Fawcett Columbine Books/Balantine Books, 1984], 3-105).
Women do some of the necessary work of mourning in the experience of meno-

pause. Men too need some way to mourn their aging process, their loss of youth. For a study of the aging process in men see Daniel Levinson, *Seasons of a Man's Life* (New York: Knopf, 1978), 191-201.

[29] Eliot Jacques, "Death and the Mid-Life Crisis," in *Death: Interpretations*, ed. H.M. Ruitenbeek (New York: Delta Books, 1969), 148-149.

[30] William James, *Varieties of Religious Experience* (New York: Mentor Edition, 1958), 99.

[31] Fritz Perls, *Ego, Hunger, and Aggression* (New York: Vintage Books), 96-97.

[32] Deuel, 63-64.

[33] R. Kastenbaum and R. Aisenberg, *Psychology of Death* (New York: Springer, 1972), 52.

[34] Deuel, 17-18.

[35] Paul Tillich, "The Theology of Pastoral Care," *Pastoral Psychology* 10, no. 97 (October 1959): 22.

[36] Along with mortality many religions have posited a theology of and view of immortality. For study on the theme of immortality see the following: Richard Kalish, *Death, Grief, and Caring Relationships* (Monterey, CA: Brooks/Cole Publishing Company, 1988), 100-116.

[37] Howard Clinebell, *op. cit.*, 231-232. Elisabeth Kübler-Ross speaks about acceptance as an experience for the dying person. Elisabeth Kübler-Ross, *On Death and Dying* (New York: Macmillan, 1969), 112-137.

[38] Therese Rando, *Loss and Anticipatory Grief* (Lexington, MA: Lexington Books, 1983), 29-34. Dr. Edwin Sneidman cautions against putting dying people in a neat series of stages and challenges us not to fall into this trap. Edwin Shneidman, *Voices of Death* (New York: Bantam Books, 1982), 108. According to Wayne Oates, people shift back and forth between denying and accepting their dying. Wayne Oates, *Pastoral Care and Counseling in Grief and Separation* (Philadelphia: Fortress Press, 1976), 20.

[39] Wayne Oates, *Pastoral Care and Counseling in Grief and Separation* (Philadelphia: Fortress Press, 1976), 16-17.

[40] Pope John Paul II, "On the Health Care Apostolate," *The Ministry of Healing — Readings in the Catholic Health Care Ministry* (St. Louis, MO: The Catholic Health Association of the United States, 1981), 2.

[41] Charles Gusmer, *And You Visited Me: Sacramental Ministry to the Sick and Dying* (New York: Pueblo Publishing Co., 1984), 139, 148-150.

[42] John B. Hesch, *Clinical Pastoral Care for Hospitalized Children and Their Families* (New York: Paulist Press, 1987), 182-185.

[43] Benedict Ashley and Kevin O'Rourke, *Health Care Ethics: A Theological Analysis* (St. Louis, MO: The Catholic Health Association, 1978), 395-396.

[44] *Ibid.*, 398. On the topic of hospital chaplaincy see: Lawrence Holst, ed., *Hospital Ministry: The Role of the Chaplain Today* (New York: Crossroad, 1985), 3-242.

[45] Kenneth Mitchell, *Hospital Chaplain* (Philadelphia: Westminster Press, 1966), quoted in Benedict Ashley and Kevin O'Rourke, *Health Care Ethics: A Theological Analysis* (St. Louis, MO: The Catholic Health Association, 1978), 402. James Empereur discusses how a real concern for the sick comes from one's lived experience in *Prophetic Anointing: God's Call to the Sick, the Elderly, and the Dying*, vol. 7, *Message of the Sacraments* (Wilmington, DE: Michael Glazier, Inc., 1982), 205-206.

[46] Ashley and O'Rourke, 402.

[47] Kenneth R. Mitchell and Herbert Anderson, *All Our Losses, All Our Griefs: Resources for Pastoral Care*, 117.

[48] Dr. Karl Menninger, quoted in Kenneth Mitchell and Herbert Anderson, *All Our Losses, All Our Griefs*, 133.

[49] Kenneth Mitchell and Herbert Anderson, *All Our Losses, All Our Griefs*, 138.

Chapter 2

[1] Bertha G. Simos, *A Time to Grieve: Loss as a Universal Human Experience* (New York: Family Service Association of America, 1979), 1.

[2] *Ibid.*, 1-2. Characteristics of loss are described by Bertha Simos in her work *A Time to Grieve: Loss as a Universal Human Experience* (New York: Family Service Association of America, 1979), 2-3. Two lists depict the multiplicity, diversity and complexity of loss. The author covers both the internal and external aspects of loss. (See John Schneider, *Stress, Loss, and Grief: Understanding Their Origins and Growth Potential* [Baltimore: University Park Press, 1983], 32, 36).

[3] Erich Lindemann, "The Symptomatology and Management of Acute Grief," *American Journal of Psychiatry* 101 (1944): 141-148.

[4] Simos, 3.

[5] *Ibid.*, 6-8

[6] *Ibid.*, 4.

[7] James Lynch, *The Broken Heart: The Medical Consequences of Loneliness* (New York: Basic Books, 1977), quoted in Bertha G. Simos, *A Time to Grieve: Loss as a Universal Human Experience* (New York: Family Service Association of America, 1979), 4.

[8] Simos, 4-5.

[9] Simos, 8.

[10] Kenneth R. Mitchell and Herbert Anderson, *All Our Losses, All Our Griefs: Resources for Pastoral Care* (Philadelphia: Westminster Press, 1983), 35.

[11] Kenneth Mitchell and Herbert Anderson, 37-38.

[12] *Ibid.*, 41-42.

[13] Simos, 11.

[14] Mitchell and Anderson, 40.

[15] Simos, 13.

[16] *Ibid.*, 12-13.

[17] Mitchell and Anderson, 43.

[18] *Ibid.*, 44.

[19] *Ibid.*, 45. Ira Tanner studied case histories of 100 clients in regards to the following "everyday" losses: personal loss, relationship loss, geographical loss, career loss, environmental loss, institutional loss, property loss, competitive loss, and seasonal loss. Ira J. Tanner, *Healing the Pain of Everyday Loss* (Minneapolis, MN: Winston Press, 1976), 54-55.
For more on developmental changes, the following work treats some of the issues involved in these transitions: Daniel Levinson, *The Seasons of a Man's Life* (New York: Knopf, 1978), 50-51.

[20] Jeroid Roussell, Jr., *I've Got the Time* (Bend, OR: Anmchara Cruces, Inc., 1996).

[21] Thomas Holmes and Minoru Masuda, "Psychosomatic Syndrome," *Psychology Today* (April 1972): 71-72, quoted in Ira Tanner, *Healing the Pain of Everyday Loss* (Minneapolis, MN: Winston Press, 1976), 60-61.

[22] Dr. Richard Rahe, quoted in Ira Tanner, *Healing the Pain of Everyday Loss* (Minneapolis, MN: Winston Press, 1976), 62.

[23] Holmes and Masuda, 72, quoted in Tanner, 62.

[24] Thomas Holmes and Minoru Masuda, *op. cit.*, 62.
For a detailed chart of these life events with their ranking and mean values, see the research of Thomas Holmes and Minoru Masuda, 63-64.

[25] M. Friedman and R. Rosenman, *Type A Behavior and Your Heart* (New York: Knopf, 1974); J. Gill, "Type A Behavior in Christian Life," *Human Development* 2 (Fall 1981): 32-41.
A person's belief systems are tied to the development of cancer and its etiology. (O.C. Simonton and S. Simonton, "Belief Systems and the management of the emotional aspects of malignancy," *Journal of Transpersonal Psychology* 7, no. 1 [1975]: 29-47).
Dr. Carl Simonton, M.D. and others detail the multi-faceted/multi-modal causes of illness particularly cancer. O.C. Simonton, Stephanie Matthews-Simonton, and James Creighton, *Getting Well Again* (New York: Bantam Books, 1978), 33-45.

[26] Dr. Sherwin Nuland, M.D. and Dr. Leon Eisenberg, quoted in Melvin Konner, M.D., *Medicine at the Crossroads-The Crisis in Health Care* (New York: Pantheon Books, 1993), 10-11.

[27] R. Scott Sullender, *Losses in Later Life: A New Way of Walking With God* (New York: Integration Books, Paulist Press, 1989), 26.

Herbert Anderson speaks of the painful process of letting go of one's children. Herbert Anderson, *Family and Pastoral Care* (Philadelphia: Fortress Press, 1984), 63-64.

[28] John Schneider, *op. cit.*, 219.

[29] R. Scott Sullender, 16.

[30] Paul Tournier, *Learn to Grow Old* (New York: Harper and Row, 1972), 184-185.

[31] Robert Peck "Psychological Developments in the Second Half of Life," *Middle Age and Aging*, ed. Bernice Neugarten, 89, quoted in R. Scott Sullender, *Losses in Later Life: A New Way of Walking With God* (New York: Integration Books, Paulist Press, 1989), 67.

[32] R. Scott Sullender, 131.

[33] *Ibid.*, 140.

[34] *Ibid.*, 141. For more on the theme of suffering particularly a "Theology of Suffering" see pp. 48-51 in Chapter Three below.

[35] Melvin Konner, 179-181.

[36] Evelyn Eaton Whitehead, "Religious Images of Aging: An Examination of Themes in Contemporary Christian Thought," *Aging and the Human Spirit: A Reader in Religion and Gerontology*, eds. Carol Le Fevre and Perry Le Fevre (Chicago: Exploration Press, 1981), 56-67.
Erik Erikson looks at the concept of identity. He equates identity with the forming of an invigorating sameness and continuity. Erik Erikson, *Identity, Youth and Crisis* (New York: W.W. Norton and Co., 1968), 19.

The theme of kenosis is covered in the "Theology of Incarnation" and the "Theology of Cross" see pp. 41-48 in Chapter Three below.

[37] R. Scott Sullender, 160. The whole theme of *Losses in Later Life* deals with various issues in aging such as: the loss of youth, the loss of family, the loss of parents, the loss of work, the loss of spouse, the loss of health, the loss of identity and the art of suffering.

How we are involved with our aging parents prepares us for our own aging. This theme is treated by Leo Misinne, a professor at the University of Nebraska, in a lecture entitled "Adventure in Aging Workshop" (Pilgrim Place, Claremont, California: August 8, 1986).

God's love is the source of our significance and not human achievement alone. (Evelyn Eaton Whitehead and James D. Whitehead, "Retirement," *Ministry with the Aging: Design, Challenges, Foundations*, ed., William M. Clements [New York: Harper and Row, 1981], 133).

[38] Viorst, 34. Gregory Rochlin talks about the loss of the mother-child connection as bringing with it abandonment issues. The child goes through all kinds of lengths to avoid feeling unwanted and rejected. Gregory Rochlin, *Griefs and Discontents: The Forces of Change* (Boston: Little, Brown, and Co., 1965), quoted in Bertha Simos, *A Time to Grieve*, 22.

For further study about attachment and its distinction with dependency, see John Bowlby, *The Making and Breaking of Affectional Bonds* (London: Tavistock Publications, 1979), 2, 130-131.

[39] John Schneider, *op. cit.*, 61.

Gerald May writes on this theme of the loss of an attachment with its associated pain in his book *Addiction and Grace* (San Francisco: Harper and Row Publishers, 1988), 96-97.

John Bowlby, Margaret Mahler, and Rene Spitz and others have each studied the separation-individuation phase of development and have demonstrated the impact of separation on small children. John Bowlby, "Separation Anxiety," *The International Journal of Psychoanalysis* 41 (1960): 7-113; M. Mahler, *On Human Symbiosis and the Vicissitudes of Individuation* (New York: International Universities Press, 1968), 1-271; and R. Spitz, "Anxiety In Infancy: A study of its manifestations in the first year of life," *International Journal of Psychoanalysis* 31 (1950): 138-143.

[40] *Ibid.*, 61.

[41] William Shakespeare, *Macbeth,* Act 4, Scene 3.

[42] Schneider, 60 and 67 with accompanying figure depicting bereavement: a (w)holistic framework.

[43] *Ibid.*, 150.

[44] *Ibid.*, 151.

[45] *Ibid.*, 150, 151.

[46] *Ibid.*, 67.

[47] *Ibid.*, 70. Hans Selye's study of alarm, the general adaptation syndrome, points out how a person is mobilized for either a 'fight or flight' reaction. Both responses are stress filled. Hans Selye, *The Stress of Life*, rev. ed. (New York: MacGraw-Hill Book Company, Inc., 1976), quoted in Walt Schafer, *Stress, Distress, and Growth* (Davis, CA: International Dialogue Press, 1978), 38-40.

For more on holding on and letting go strategies see Schneider, 125ff and 138-140.

John Schneider produces two lists of the consequences of prolonged use of holding on and letting go strategies. John Schneider, *Stress, Loss, and Grief: Understanding Their Origins and Growth Potential* (Baltimore: University Park Press, 1983), 150, 151.

[48] *Ibid.*, 104-107. John Schneider reviews the topic of people telling their stories of loss. (*Ibid.*, 113).

[49] *Ibid.*, 162-163, 164-166, 167, 168, and 170.

[50] *Ibid.*, 179-180, 184, 187, and 188.

[51] *Ibid.*, 202-204.

[52] *Ibid.*, 208, 213, 215, 218, and 219.

[53] *Ibid.*, 230-231, 235-236 including figure 14.1.

[54] Vanderlyn R. Pine, "An Agenda for Adaptive Anticipation of Bereavement," *Loss and Anticipatory Grief*, ed. Therese Rando (Lexington, MA: Lexington Books, 1986), 40.

[55] Therese Rando, "A Comprehensive Analysis of Anticipatory Grief: Perspectives, Processes, Promises, and Problems," *Loss and Anticipatory Grief*, ed. Therese Rando (Lexington, MA: Lexington Books, 1986), 24.

[56] E. Lindemann, "Symptomatology and Management of Acute Grief," *American Journal of Psychiatry* 101 (1944): 147.

[57] E.M. Pattison, "The Living-Dying Process," *Psychosocial Care of the Dying Patient*, ed. C.A. Garfield (New York: McGraw-Hill, 1978), 159-161.

[58] Therese Rando, 27.

[59] Wayne Oates, *Your Particular Grief* (Philadelphia: Westminster Press, 1981), 41.

[60] M.J. Horowitz, et. al., "Pathological grief and the activation of latent self-images," *American Journal of Psychiatry* 137 (1980): 1157. The barriers to resolving grief are discussed by Kelduyn Garland in "Unresolved Grief," *Neonatal Network* (December 1986): 29-37.

[61] William Worden, *Grief Counseling and Grief Therapy: A Handbook for the Mental Health Practitioner* (New York: Springer Publishing Co.), 53-57.

[62] *Ibid.*, 58-61.

[63] Donald Sutherland, *The Rosary Murders*, produced by Robert Laurel and Michael Mahlic, 105 minutes, Virgin Vision, 1987, videocassette.

[64] Charles Kessler, "AIDS and Pastoral Care," *Making Chaplaincy Work: Practical Approaches*, ed. Burton Laurel Arthur (New York: Haworth Press, 1988), 49-58.

[65] Bertha Simos, 211-213. Jean Shinoda Bolen in *Goddesses in Everywoman — A New Psychology of Women* speaks of the need to shed cultural stereotypes. Women choose meaning through their recovery from vulnerable inner archetypes and outer passive stereotypes. Jean Shinoda Bolen, *Goddesses in Everywoman — A New Psychology of Women* (San Francisco: Harper and Row, Publishers, 1984), 4, 280-281.

[66] Edgar Jackson, *The Many Faces of Grief* (Nashville, TN: Abingdon Press, 1977), 99-100.

[67] *Ibid.*, 104.

[68] *Ibid.*, 131.

Chapter 3

[1] Patrick V. Ahern, *Maurice & Thérèse: The Story of a Love* (New York: Doubleday, 1998), 63.

[2] Bruce Metzger and Roland Murphy, eds., *The New Oxford Annotated Bible with the Apocrypha — New Revised Standard Version, An Ecumenical Study Bible, Completely Revised and Enlarged* (New York: Oxford University Press, 1991), 385, NT.

[3] Howard Clinebell and Martha Hickman, *Growing Through Grief: Personal Healing, Program I — The Five Tasks of Grief*, produced by United Methodist Communications, 60 minutes, 1983, videocassette.

[4] Maurice Freedman, "The Healing Dialogue in Psychotherapy," *The Journal of Religious Psychology* (1985): 199.

[5] *Ibid.*, 199-200. For further study on the empathic way of being see Carl Rogers, *A Way of Being* (Boston: Houghton Mifflin Company, 1980), 137-161.

[6] Carl Rogers, *A Way of Being* (Boston: Houghton Mifflin Company, 1980), 142f. Adrian van Kaam discusses the need to leave one's self-centered world of daily involvement including one's pre-occupation with personal desires and professional pride. This embodies the incarnational stance of entering the world of the other through shedding one's own conscious and unconscious preconceptions. Adrian van Kaam, *The Art of Existential Counseling* (Wilkes-Barres, PA: Dimension Books, 1966), 23.

[7] *Ibid.*, 142f.

[8] William B. Oglesby, Jr., *Biblical Themes for Pastoral Care and Counseling* (Nashville, TN: Abingdon Press, 1980), 28.

[9] *Ibid.*, 28.

[10] George Maloney, *Listen, Prophets!* (Denville, NJ: Dimension Books, 1974), 80.

[11] William Oglesby, Jr., 28-29. Joseph Campbell speaks of the heart as the person's consciousness which in death is joined to God Who is All Consciousness. Joseph Campbell, *The Power of Myth with Bill Moyers, The First Storytellers Program*, produced by Mystic Fire Video, Inc., 60 minutes, 1988, videocassette.

[12] *Ibid.*, 29.

[13] Adolf Guggenbuhl-Craig, *Power in the Helping Professions* (Dallas, TX: Spring Publications, Inc., 1971), 12-19.

[14] Eugene Kennedy from his notes on "Characteristics of the Counselor," *On Becoming a Counselor* (New York: Continuum, 1975), 1-55.

[15] Ethical decision-making is discussed as a topic in the following reference books: Benedict Ashley and Kevin O'Rourke, *Ethics of Health Care* (St. Louis, MO: The Catholic Health Association of the United States, 1986), 29-34, 54, 66-68, 71, and 81-104; and Benedict Ashley and Kevin O'Rourke, *Health Care Ethics — A Theological Analysis*, 2d ed. (St. Louis, MO: The Catholic Health Association of the United States, 1982), 56-61, 66-67, 69-72, 83, 123-124, 126-127, 136 and 148-175.

[16] Bruce Metzger and Roland Murphy, eds., *op. cit.*, 78, NT.

[17] Susanne Heine, *Matriarchs, Goddesses, and Images of God: A Critique of a Feminist Theology* (Minneapolis, MN: Augsburg, 1988), 138-139.

[18] G. von Rad, *Old Testament Theology* 2 (New York: Harper and Row, 1962), 19.

[19] Thomas Aquinas, *Summa Theologica*, pt. 1, q. 92, art. 1, 2; q. 99, art. 2; pt. 3, supp. q. 39.1, quoted in Rosemary Radford Ruether, *Sexism and God-Talk*, 126.

[20] Anne Carr, *Transforming Grace: Christian Tradition and Women's Experience* (San Francisco: Harper and Row, 1988), 163.

[21] Carr, 152. Susanne Heine treats of the incarnational, biblical, maternal images of God in *Matriarchs, Goddesses, and Images of God: A Critique of a Feminist Theology* (Minneapolis, MN: Augsburg, 1988), 10-40.

[22] Jack Wintz, ed., "The Pope's Mission Encyclical Condensed — The Mission of Christ the Redeemer — Key Passages of Pope John Paul II's '*Redemptoris Missio*': On the Permanent Validity of the Church's Missionary Mandate," *Catholic Update* (Cincinnati, OH: St. Anthony Messenger Press, October 1991), 2.

[23] Wintz, ed., 2.

[24] Paul Tournier, *A Doctor's Casebook* (Valley Forge, PA: SCM Press Ltd., 1966), 44.

[25] Bruce Metzger and Roland Murphy, eds., *op. cit.*, 88, NT.

[26] Walter Brueggemann, *Prophetic Imagination* (Philadelphia: Fortress Press, 1978), 112.

[27] Bruce Metzger and Roland Murphy, eds., *op. cit.*, 6, NT.

[28] Karl Rahner, *Foundations of Christian Faith: An Introduction to the Idea of Christianity*, trans. William Dych (New York: Crossroad, 1978), 284.

[29] Edward Schillebeeckx, *Jesus: An Experiment in Christology*, trans. Hubert Hoskins (New York: Crossroad, 1979), 640-641. For additional study on the humanity of Jesus read Roch A. Kereszty, O. Cist., "The Humanity of the Son" in *Jesus Christ: Fundamentals of Christology* (New York: Alba House, 1991), 321-334.

[30] Hans Küng, *The Incarnation of God: An Introduction to Hegel's Theological Thought as Prolegomena to a Future Christology*, trans. J.R. Stephenson (New York: Crossroad Publishing Co., 1987), 162ff. Jurgen Moltmann develops a detailed treatment of the theology of the Cross including Christological, soteriological, and eschatological themes. Jurgen Moltmann, *The Crucified God: The Cross of Christ as the Foundation and Criticism of Christian Theology* (San Francisco: Harper Collins Publishers, 1974), 205. A detailed treatment of Jesus' passion and death on the cross is further elaborated in this work: Donald Senior, *The Passion of Jesus in the Gospel of Mark* (Wilmington, DE: Michael Glazier, Inc., 1984), 1-158.

[31] Bruce Metzger and Roland Murphy, eds., *op. cit.*, 260, NT.

[32] Eberhard Jungel, *God as the Mystery of the World: On the Foundation of the Theology of the Crucified One in the Dispute between Theism and Atheism*, trans. Darrell L. Guder (Grand Rapids: Eerdmans, 1983), 206, quoted in Douglas John Hall, *God and Human Suffering*, 106. In Luke's version of the passion, Jesus resists the temptation to follow ways of power, force and violence, and God vindicates Jesus raising him from the dead. The cross of Jesus calls professionals to be liberators, not getting caught in any form of coercion in positions of authority. (Joseph Grassi, *God Makes Me Laugh: A New Approach to Luke* [Wilmington, DE: Michael Glazier, 1986], 139-140).

[33] Lawrence Holst, "A Ministry of Paradox in a Place of Paradox," *Hospital Ministry: The Role of The Chaplain Today*, ed. Lawrence Holst (New York: Crossroad, 1985), 9. In *The Minister as Diagnostician: Personal Problems in Pastoral Perspective*, Paul Pruyser writes about the complex and multidimensional aspects of pain and suffering that often cry out for enlightenment and resolution through several perspectives at once (Philadelphia: Westminster, 1976), 51. Elsewhere, Terence Fretheim narrates how God suffers to mend the breach between the Divine and the human (*The Suffering of God: An Old Testament Perspective* [Philadelphia: Fortress Press, 1984], 107-148).

34 C.S. Song, *The Compassionate God* (Maryknoll, NY: Orbis, 1982), 115, quoted in Douglas John Hall, *God and Human Suffering*, 116.

35 Douglas John Hall, 121 and 123-147. These pages deal with the Church as a community of suffering and hope. The Church participates in the sufferings of Christ and becomes transformed into the image and body of Christ. The Roman Catholic Bishops of Oregon and Washington in *Living and Dying Well* discuss the theme of suffering and dying. The pastoral letter emphasizes the importance of the Church's call to reach out to people in their dying. During this time people need to be given care and comfort when curing no longer works (Bishops of the Oregon Catholic Conference and the Washington State Catholic Conference, *Living and Dying Well: A Pastoral Letter about the End of Life* [October 1991], 9-11).

36 Harshajan Pazhayatil, *Counseling in Health Care* (Chicago: Franciscan Herald Press, 1977), 210. Richard Vieth pursues the theme of innocent suffering in his work *Holy Power, Human Pain* (Bloomington, IN: Meyer, Stone, and Company, 1988), 110-137. The following works likewise study the question of evil: Robert Doran, "Jungian Psychology and Spirituality: III," ed. Robert Moore, *Carl Jung and Christian Spirituality* (New York: Paulist Press, 1988), 103-107; John Sanford, "The Problem of Evil in Christianity and Analytical Psychology," *Carl Jung and Christian Spirituality*, ed. Robert Moore (New York: Paulist Press, 1988), 109-130.
Compassionate pastoral care — to the elderly, who are suffering — ought to address issues of meaning and directionality (life review), growth and directionality, and suffering and service. (Albert Meiburg, "Pastoral Care with the Aged: The Spiritual Dimension," *Spiritual Dimension of Pastoral Care: Witness to the Ministry of Wayne Oates*, eds. Gerald Borchert and Andrew Lester [Philadelphia: Westminster, 1985], 97-100).

37 Lawrence Holst, *op. cit.*, 9.

38 Cornelius J. Van Der Poel, "Suffering and Healing: The Process of Growth," *The Ministry of Healing* (St. Louis, MO: The Catholic Health Association of the United States, 1981), 47.

39 *Ibid.*, 47-48.

40 Henri Nouwen, *The Wounded Healer* (Garden City, NY: Doubleday, 1965), 1-100. Adolf Guggenbuhl-Craig's book discusses the helper's negative and destructive inner fantasies and their impact on a therapeutic relationship. Adolf Guggenbuhl-Craig, *Power in the Helping Professions* (Dallas, TX: Spring Publications, Inc.), 50-51.

41 *Ibid.*, 1-100.

42 Bruce Metzger and Roland Murphy, eds., *op. cit.*, 366, NT.

43 James Emerson, *Suffering: Its Meaning and Ministry* (Nashville, TN: Abingdon Press, 1986), 117 and 125.

44 *Ibid.*, 133.

45 Dorothee Soelle, *Suffering*, trans. R. Kalin (Philadelphia: Fortress Press, 1975), 98.

46 R. Scott Sullender, *Grief and Growth: Pastoral Resources for Emotional and Spiritual Growth* (New York: Paulist Press, 1985), 89.

47 Kenneth Mitchell and Herbert Anderson, *All Our Losses, All Our Griefs: Resources for Pastoral Care* (Philadelphia: Westminster, 1983), 165-167.

48 Joseph Grassi, *God Makes Me Laugh: A New Approach to Luke* (Wilmington, DE: Michael Glazier, 1986), 144.

49 Robert Karris, *Invitation To Luke: A Commentary on the Gospel of Luke with Complete Text from The Jerusalem Bible* (Garden City, NY: Image Books, 1977), 273.

Jesus is for all people especially the disadvantaged: sinners, sick, women, poor and Samaritans and Gentiles. For further study on this topic refer to Robert O'Toole's work *The Unity of Luke's Theology: An Analysis of Luke-Acts*, Vol. 9, *Good News Studies* (Wilmington, DE: Michael Glazier, Inc., 1984), 109-148.

Feminist Christian theologians elaborate on the theme of inclusiveness expressed in the Incarnation, Cross/Death and Resurrection of Jesus Christ. June O'Connor states that Jesus undercuts the predominant mode of human relating and the foundational unit of society at his time: the first century Graeco-Roman male-favored patriarchal household. See June O'Connor, "Feminism and Christology," *Newsletter of the Currents in Contemporary Christology Group of the AAR* (Fall 1986): 14.

[50] Donald Senior, *Invitation To Matthew: A Commentary on the Gospel of Matthew with Complete Text from the Jerusalem Bible* (Garden City, NY: Image Books, 1978), 276. For further study see the following works: Jack Dean Kingsbury, *Matthew*, ed. Gerhard Krodel, *Proclamation Commentaries* (Philadelphia: Fortress Press, 1977), 101. Norman Perrin shows how Matthew portrays Jesus' Resurrection as an inauguration of the age of the Church in the world in *Resurrection According to Matthew, Mark, and Luke* (Philadelphia: Fortress Press, 1977), 55.

[51] Donald Senior, *The Passion of Jesus in the Gospel of Mark*, vol. 2, *The Passion Series* (Wilmington, DE: Michael Glazier, Inc., 1984), 137. For further study see the following works: Wilfrid Harrington, *Mark*, Vol. 4, *New Testament Message* (Wilmington, DE: Michael Glazier, Inc., 1984), 243-244; Eduard Schweizer, *The Good News According to Mark*, trans. Donald Madvig (Atlanta, GA: John Knox Press, 1976), 363ff. Norman Perrin summarizes the impact of Christ's Resurrection in Mark's Gospel: "Jesus is experienced as Risen, transforming one's daily life" (Norman Perrin, *The Resurrection According to Matthew, Mark, and Luke* [Philadelphia: Fortress Press, 1977], 38).

[52] Eugene LaVerdiere, *Luke*, Vol. 5, *New Testament Message* (Wilmington, DE: Michael Glazier, Inc., 1980), 287. According to Norman Perrin, the Lukan resurrection narratives challenge the disciple to think in terms of imitating Jesus. One accepts responsibility for the gospel of Jesus as Jesus accepted responsibility for his mission. The disciple lives in the power of the same Spirit which empowered Jesus (Norman Perrin, *The Resurrection According to Matthew, Mark and Luke* [Philadelphia: Fortress Press, 1977], 76-77).

[53] O'Toole, 49-51.

[54] Raymond Brown, *The Gospel According to John, XIII-XXI: A Translation with Commentary*, Vol. 29A, *The Anchor Bible* (Garden City, NY: Doubleday and Company, Inc., 1970), 1015-1016. According to Robert Kysar, the Risen Jesus gives the Holy Spirit with peace. This eschatological peace is given as a sign of the believer's new life in the newly formed creation of God. Robert Kysar, *John: Augsburg Commentary on the New Testament* (Minneapolis, MN: Augsburg, 1986), 303-305.

[55] Raymond Brown, *The Community of the Beloved Disciple: The Life, Loves and Hates of an Individual Church in New Testament Times* (New York: Paulist Press, 1979), 131-132.

[56] Robert Kysar, *John, the Maverick Gospel* (Atlanta, GA: John Knox Press, 1976), 99-100.

[57] Bruce Metzger and Roland Murphy, eds., *op. cit.*, 153, NT.

[58] Douglas John Hall, *Christian Mission: The Stewardship of Life in the Kingdom of Death* (New York: Friendship Press, 1985), 79.

[59] *Ibid.*, 93-94.

[60] *Ibid.*, 99.

[61] Jurgen Moltmann, *Theology of Hope: On the Ground and the Implications of a Christian Eschatology* (New York: Harper and Row, 1967), 158.

[62] Bruce Metzger and Roland Murphy, eds., *op. cit.*, 385, NT.

Chapter 4

[1] Bruce Metzger and Roland Murphy, eds., *op. cit.*, 144, NT.

[2] *Ibid.*

[3] Irene Moriarty, "Sudden Death: Pastoral Presence with the Bereaved," *Resources for Ministry in Death and Dying*, eds. Larry Platt and Roger Branch (Nashville, TN: Broadman, 1988), 227.

[4] Henri Nouwen, *Reaching Out* (Garden City, NY: Doubleday and Co., Inc., 1975), 51. William Avery draws on the description of presence from two religious existentialists, Martin Buber and Gabriel Marcel in fleshing out the ministry of presence. William Avery, "Toward an Understanding of Ministry of Presence," *The Journal of Pastoral Care,* Vol. XL, No. 4 (Dec. 1986), 342-353.

[5] Sheila Cassidy, *Sharing the Darkness: The Spirituality of Caring* (London: Darton, Longman and Todd, 1988), 5.

[6] David Augsburger, *Pastoral Counseling Across Cultures* (Philadelphia: Westminster Press, 1986), 37.

[7] *Ibid.*, 37.

[8] *Ibid.*, 38.

[9] Melanie Klein, "Mourning and Its Relation to Manic-Depressive States," *International Journal of Psychoanalysis* XXI (1940), 127-128.

[10] Bernard Lonergan, *Method in Theology* (New York: Herder and Herder, 1972), 112-115.

[11] Gordon Allport, "The Historical Background of Modern Social Psychology," *Handbook of Social Psychology*, ed. G. Lindzey, Vol. 1 (Cambridge, MA: Addison-Wesley Publishing Co., 1954), 13.

[12] Terence Fretheim, *The Suffering of God: An Old Testament Perspective* (Philadelphia: Fortress Press, 1984), 63, 68.

[13] Edward Thornton, "Finding Center in Pastoral Care," *Spiritual Dimensions of Pastoral Care: Witness to the Ministry of Wayne E. Oates*, eds. Gerald Borchert and Andrew Lester (Philadelphia: Westminster Press, 1985), 20.

[14] Cecilia Baranowski, "Stroke: Its Mechanics and Dynamics in Ministry to Patients," *Making Chaplaincy Work: Practical Approaches*, ed. Laurel Arthur Burton (New York: The Haworth Press, 1988), 87.

[15] *Ibid.*, 88.

[16] William Clinebell, Jr., *op. cit.*, 67-68.

[17] James Fowler structures and hypothesizes his *Stages of Faith* through utilizing Jean Piaget, Lawrence Kohlberg, Daniel Levinson, Carol Gilligan and other theorists. James Fowler, *Stages of Faith: The Psychology of Human Development and the Quest for Meaning* (New York: Harper and Row, 1981), 1-200.

[18] Clinebell, Jr., 103.

[19] Bernard J. Tyrrell, "Christotherapy: An Approach to Facilitating Psychospiritual

Healing Growth," *Clinical Handbook of Pastoral Counseling*, eds. Robert Wicks, Richard Parsons, and Donald Capps (New York: Integration Books, Paulist Press, 1985), 58.

[20] *Ibid.*, 59.

[21] Bernard Lonergan, *Method in Theology* (New York: Herder and Herder, 1972), 238-240. For Bernard Lonergan this project of self-appropriation moves through five levels of human operations and consciousness toward a greater degree of interiority (Bernard Lonergan, *Method in Theology* [New York: Herder and Herder, 1972], Chapters One and Four, quoted in Robert Doran, "Jungian Psychology and Christian Spirituality: I," *Carl Jung and Christian Spirituality*, ed. Robert Moore [New York: Paulist Press, 1988], 78-79). Robert Doran discusses the subject of intellectual conversion in his work *Subject and Psyche: Ricoeur, Jung, and the Search for Foundations* (Washington, DC: University Press of America, 1977), 240-246.

[22] Tyrrell, 59. Psychic conversion and self-transcendent interiority is discussed in this study. (See also Robert Doran, *Subject and Psyche: Ricoeur, Jung, and the Search for Foundations* [Washington, DC: University Press of America, 1977], 74).

[23] Tyrrell, 62.

[24] *Ibid.*, 63.

[25] *Ibid.*, 63-64.

[26] Robert Doran, "Jungian Psychology and Christian Spirituality: I," 72.

[27] Michael Crosby, *Spirituality of the Beatitudes: Matthew's Challenge for First World Christians* (Maryknoll, NY: Orbis Books, 1981), 75-76.

[28] Joann Wolski Conn, *Women's Spirituality: Resources for Christian Development* (New York: Paulist Press, 1986), 1-5.

[29] Anne Carr, *Transforming Grace: Christian Tradition and Women's Experience* (San Francisco: Harper and Row, 1988), 208.

[30] *Ibid.*, 208.

[31] Edward Thornton, "Finding Center in Pastoral Care," *Spiritual Dimensions of Pastoral Care: Witness to the Ministry of Wayne E. Oates*, eds. Gerald Borchert and Andrew Lester (Philadelphia: Westminster Press, 1985), 20.

[32] *Ibid.*, 20.

[33] *Ibid.*, 20.

[34] Benedict Groeschel, *Spiritual Passages: The Psychology of Spiritual Development* (New York: Crossroad, 1983), 186. This transformation process is described in Kevin Culligan's *Spiritual Direction: Contemporary Readings*. It is a process toward full absorption and integration into the life of the Spirit at the deepest center of the soul; the process is one of ever deepening cycles of self-consciousness, surrender and union. Kevin Culligan, *Spiritual Direction: Contemporary Readings* (Locust Valley, NY: Living Flame Press, 1983), 146.

[35] Teilhard de Chardin, "Pantheism and Christianity" in *Christianity and Evolution* (New York: Harcourt Brace Jovanovich, Inc., 1969), 73-74.

[36] Gerald May, *Will and Spirit: A Contemplative Psychology* (San Francisco: Harper and Row, 1982), 321.

[37] Douglas John Hall, *Christian Mission: The Stewardship of Life in the Kingdom of Death* (New York: Fortress Press, 1985), 47.

[38] Francis Nemeck and Marie Coombs, *The Way of Spiritual Direction, Consecrated Life Studies*, 5 (Wilmington, DE: Michael Glazier, Inc., 1985), 34. The qualities of a

spiritual guide are outlined in Kenneth Leech's *Soul Friend*. The author speaks of holiness of life, closeness to God, experience of the realities of prayer, knowledge of Scripture, great writings of spirituality, discernment and submissiveness to the Holy Spirit. Kenneth Leech, *Soul Friend: The Practice of Christian Spirituality* (San Francisco: Harper and Row, 1987), 88-89.

39 *Ibid.*, 43.

40 *Ibid.*, 56.

41 Howard Clinebell, *Growth Counseling: Hope Centered Methods of Actualizing Human Wholeness* (Nashville, TN: Abingdon Press, 1979), 123.

Chapter Five

1 David Augsburger, *Pastoral Counseling Across Cultures* (Philadelphia: Westminster Press, 1986), 13-35. David Augsburger talks about interpathy in which one enters the totally foreign perspective of another. It is very difficult to do this and to shed one's perceptions, stereotypes and judgments about alien values.

2 Bill Moyers, *Healing and the Mind — The Mind Body Connection,* Part 2, 60 minutes, David Grubin Productions, Inc. and Public Affairs Television, Inc., 1993, videocassette. Pastoral care assists people in dealing with the spiritual and emotional aspects of health. Studies are pointing to the ability of pastoral care to contribute to increased effectiveness of the immune system. (See Larry VandeCreek, "Can Pastoral Care Contribute to Increased Competency of the Immune System," *Chaplaincy Today* 8, no. 2 [February 1993]: 2-3).

3 *Ibid.*

4 *Ibid.*

5 *Ibid.*

6 Charles Truax and Robert Carkhuff, *Toward Effective Counseling and Psychotherapy — Training and Practice* (New York: Aldine Publishing Company, 1967), 285.

7 Bette Midler and Barbara Hershey, *Beaches*, produced by Terri Schwartz, 123 minutes, Touchstone Pictures, 1988, videocassette.

8 Elliott Dacher, *PNI Psychoneuroimmunology —The New Mind/Body Healing Program* (New York: Paragon House, 1993), 2.

9 Worden, 11-16.

10 Beverly Raphael, "Preventative Intervention with the Recently Bereaved," *Archives of General Psychiatry* 34 (1977): 1450-1454, quoted in William Worden, *Grief Counseling and Grief Therapy: A Handbook for the Mental Health Practitioner* (New York: Springer Publishing Company, 1982), 38-39.

11 Pastoral Care Department, *Bereavement Folder* (Bend, OR: St. Charles Medical Center, 1989), 1-21.

12 Roy Setziol, "Panel 9: The Dedication," *The Teak Panels* (Bend, OR: St. Charles Medical Center Lobby).

13 Sheila O'Connell-Roussell, *Anmchara: Call of the Spirit, Reflections on Pastoral Ministry* (Bend, OR: Anmchara Cruces, Inc., 1996).

14 Melody Beattie, *Codependent No More — How to Stop Controlling Others and Start Caring for Yourself* (New York: Harper and Row, 1987), 35-47.

15 Albert Ellis and Robert Harper, *A New Guide to Rational Living* (North Hollywood, CA: Wilshire Book Company, 1975), 92-95.

[16] Robert Alberti and Michael Emmons, *Your Perfect Right — A Guide to Assertive Living* (San Luis Obispo, CA: Impact Publishers, 1970), 40-42, 52.

[17] Martha Davis, Elizabeth Robbins, and Matthew McKay *The Relaxation and Stress Reduction Workbook* (Richmond, CA: New Harbinger Publications, 1980), 14-168.

[18] Dacher, 9-11.

[19] Bruce Metzger and Roland Murphy, eds., *op. cit.*, 219, NT.

[20] *Ibid.*

Appendix A

[1] Thomas Groome, *Christian Religious Education - Sharing Our Story and Vision* (San Francisco: Harper and Row, 1980), 73.

[2] James and Evelyn Whitehead, *Method in Ministry: Theological Reflection and Christian Ministry* (New York: The Seabury Press, 1980), 13-14.

[3] David Augsburger, *op. cit.*, 22-31.

[4] Charles Truax and Robert Carkhuff, *op. cit.*, 285.

[5] Gerard Egan, *The Skilled Helper: A Systematic Approach to Effective Helping*, third edition (Monterey, CA: Brooks/Cole Publishing Company, 1986), 203, 264-265; and Allen Ivey, *Intentional Interviewing and Counseling* (Monterey, CA: Brooks-Cole Publishing, 1983), 151.

[6] Eric Cassell, *The Nature of Suffering and The Goals of Medicine* (New York: Oxford University Press, 1991), 115-122, 127-137.

[7] Sharon Fish and Judith Allen Shelly, *Spiritual Care: The Nurse's Role* (Ontario, Canada: Inter-Varsity Christian Fellowship, 1978), 64, 79-81; and Greg Stoddard and Jean Burns-Haney, "Developing an Integrated Approach to Spiritual Assessment: One Department's Experience," *The Care Giver Journal* 7, no. 1 (1990): 63-86.
Nurses access the spiritual dimensions of nursing practice through pastoral resources such as prayer; Scripture, religious literature or music; clergy and chaplains, etc. (Jean Stallwood, *Clinical Nursing Pathophysiological and Psychosocial Approaches* [New York: Macmillan Publishers, 1975], 1091-1095).

[8] Sharon Fish and Judith Allen Shelly, 64.

[9] Ellison Craig and R.F. Paloutzian, "Spiritual Well-Being: Conceptualization and Measurement," *Journal of Psychology and Theology* 11, no. 4 (1983): 330-340.

[10] Mary Tyler Moore and Bernadette Peters, *The Last Best Year*, produced by David Rintels, 100 minutes, Gideon Productions, 1990, videocassette.

[11] Sally Field and Julia Roberts, *Steel Magnolias*, produced by Ray Stark, 118 minutes, Tri-Star Pictures, 1989, videocassette.

[12] Shirley MacLaine and Debra Winger, *Terms of Endearment*, produced by James L. Brooks, 132 minutes, Paramount Pictures, 1983, videocassette.

[13] Anne Bancroft and Sissy Spacek, *Night Mother*, produced by Aaron Spelling and Alan Greisman, 96 minutes, Universal Studios, Inc., 1986, videocassette.

[14] William Hurt, *The Doctor*, produced by Laura Ziskin, 123 minutes, Touchstone Pictures, 1991, videocassette. The film, *The Doctor*, deals with the insensitivity of the medical profession to those persons whom they treat. William Hurt is an insensitive and callous physician who gets cancer and comes to grips with his own vulnerability and feelings through the help of a young woman who is dying of a can-

cerous brain tumor. The movie challenges doctors to treat their patients with compassion dealing with them as persons.

[15] Howard Clinebell, Jr., *Growing Through Loss*, 60 minutes, Methodist Communication, 1983, 6 videocassettes.

[16] Patrick Del Zoppo, *Ministry to the Bereaved — Bereavement Ministry in Times of Crises*, 60 minutes, Catholic Telecommunications Network of America, 1980, 12 videocassettes. In *Almost Home* Sr. Thea Bowman's dying experience is recounted in an inspirational and personal journey through the suffering and uncertainty of terminal illness. Sr. Thea Bowman, *Almost Home: Living with Suffering and Dying*, 60 minutes, Liguori Publications, 1989, videocassette. *A Family in Grief* vividly illustrates the personal struggles that a family experienced in dealing with sudden and tragic death. Dr. Therese Rando, a bereavement therapist and author says it is one of the best films ever produced on the subject of family bereavement (*A Family in Grief: The Ameche Story*, 26 minutes, Research Press, 1987, videocassette).

[17] Howard Clinebell, Jr., *op. cit.*, 239-240.

[18] Thomas Droege, *Guided Grief Imagery: A Resource for Grief Ministry and Death Education* (New York: Paulist Press, 1985), 106-145.

[19] Worden, 110-111.

[20] Jeroid Roussell, Jr., *Role Playing Exercise/Improv* (Bend, OR: Anmchara Cruces, Inc., 1996). For extra role playing exercises on grief counseling see William Worden, *Grief Counseling and Grief Therapy*, 118-129.

[21] This tendency is entrenched in the medical approach since it emphasizes clinical examinations focusing on the diagnostic and therapeutic capacities, and not the problems of living. For further study see, Dacher, 3, 6-7.

[22] Jeanne Acterberg, *Imagery in Healing: Shamanism and Modern Medicine* (Boston, MA: Shambhala Publications, Inc. 1985), 114-115.

[23] Jeroid Roussell, Jr., "Guided Imagery Exercise: Your Death" (Bend, OR: Anmchara Cruces, Inc., 1996). For additional guided grief imagery exercises see Thomas Droege, *Guided Grief Imagery*, 131-133. Guided imagery has the advantage of freeing people experiencing loss to visualize scenes of the loss as they were happening in the present. The person does this through his/her mind's eye while keeping their eyelids closed. (Coval B. MacDonald, "Loss and Bereavement," *Clinical Handbook of Pastoral Counseling*, eds. Robert Wicks, Richard Parsons, and Donald Capps [New York: Paulist Press, 1984], 550).

[24] Lawrence LeShan, *Cancer as a Turning Point — A Handbook for People with Cancer — Their Families and Health Professionals* (New York: New American Library, Dutton, 1990), 161-165, 167.

[25] Donald Capps, *Biblical Approaches to Pastoral Counseling* (Philadelphia: Westminster Press, 1981), 47-97.

[26] Sharon Fish and Judith Allen Shelly, *Spiritual Care: The Nurse's Role* (Downers Grove, IL: InterVarsity Press, 1978), 35-54, 95-124.

[27] Leroy Joesten, "The Voices of the Dying and the Bereaved: A Bridge Between Loss and Growth," *Hospital Ministry - The Role of the Chaplain Today*, ed. Lawrence Holst (New York: Crossroad, 1987), 149.

[28] Larry Platt and Roger Branch, *Resources for Ministry in Death and Dying* (Nashville, TN: Broadman Press, 1988), 141, 142-143, 146, and 148. Pastors bring emotional and spiritual support through the use of ritual. In the absence of ritual people substitute psychotherapy as a primary way of facilitating normal grief reactions.

Rituals provide the guidance encouraging people to grieve; they provide a structure in which to grieve; and they confront the reality of loss and emotional release for grieving people — a catharsis. (R. Scott Sullender, *Grief and Growth: Pastoral Resources for Emotional and Spiritual Growth* [New York: Paulist Press, 1985], 144ff).

For further pastoral resources for grief and bereavement ministry see the following handbooks: John James and Frank Cherry, *The Grief Recovery Handbook: A Step-by-Step Program for Moving Beyond Loss* (New York: Harper and Row, 1988), 77-98; Patrick Del Zoppo, *Mourning: The Journey from Grief to Healing* (New York: Alba House, 1995), 1-43; Terence P. Curley, *Six Steps for Managing Loss* (New York: Alba House, 1998), 1-48.

Appendix C

1 Jerry and Sheila Roussell, Roger and Teri Nichols, *Meditation on The Source Within*, Roger Nichols Music, copyright 1993.

2 *Ibid.*

This book was designed and published by St. Pauls/ Alba House, the publishing arm of the Society of St. Paul, an international religious congregation of priests and brothers dedicated to serving the Church through the communications media. For information regarding this and associated ministries of the Pauline Family of Congregations, write to the Vocation Director, Society of St. Paul, 7050 Pinehurst, Dearborn, Michigan 48126 or check our internet site, www.albahouse.org